From Sea to Shining Sea for Children will turn youngsters on to history. In exciting narrative they'll hear Charles Finney as his sermons bring revival to the frontier. They'll ride in Conestoga wagons on the long journey west. They'll see the courage of the men at the Alamo and suffer with black men and women under the scourge of slavery. Through it all they will be reminded that God is faithful to His people, even as He is in the face of today's challenges.

A glossary and questions for discussion make this informative and enjoyable book a valuable teaching tool.

The first book of this series, *The Light and the Glory for Children,* recounts events in America's history from Christopher Columbus's voyage in 1492 to George Washington's inauguration in 1783. It shows how God intervened time and again in the events of early American history to accomplish His grand plan for a very special place where his followers could worship freely.

Just as your children will enjoy *The Light and the Glory for Children* and *From Sea to Shining Sea for Children,* you're sure to appreciate the enlightening best-sellers on which they are based:

The Light and the Glory

Peter Marshall and David Manuel trace God's plan for America from the fruition of Columbus's dream to Washington's inauguration.

From Sea to Shining Sea

Peter Marshall and David Manuel present a powerful sequel that chronicles God's intervention in American history from Washington's presidency to the brink of the Civil War.

These two dynamic and enlightening accounts of American history show the part God played in our past and challenge Americans to make our country what He intended from the beginning.

From SEA to SHINING SEA

For Children

Discovering God's Plan for America in Her First Half-Century of Independence 1787-1837

Peter Marshall
&
David Manuel

with
Anna Wilson Fishel

Fleming H. Revell
A Division of Baker Book House Co
Grand Rapids, Michigan 49516

Copyright © 1993 by Peter Marshall and David Manuel

Published by Fleming H. Revell
a division of Baker Book House Company
P.O. Box 6287, Grand Rapids, MI 49516-6287

Fifth printing, October 1994

Printed in the United States of America

Book development by March Media, Inc.

Library of Congress Cataloging–in–Publication Data

Fishel, Anna Wilson.
    From sea to shining sea for children: discovering God's plan for America in her first half–century of independence, 1787–1837/Peter Marshall and David Manuel: adapted by Anna Wilson Fishel.
    p. cm.
    ISBN 0-8007-5484-0
    1. United States—History—1787-1837—Juvenile literature. 2. United States—Social conditions—To 1837—Juvenile literature. 3. United States—Church history—19th century—Juvenile literature. 4. History (Theology)—Juvenile literature. 5. Providence and government of God—Juvenile literature. I. Marshall, Peter, 1940- From sea to shining sea. II. Title.
E302.F53 1993
973—dc20   93-10801

The material in this book has been carefully researched and is historically accurate, but specific scenes and conversations have been fictionalized to heighten the drama and foster its readability. Direct quotations of historic personages are taken from the standard edition of From Sea to Shining Sea and the sources are footnoted there.

Scripture quotations are from the New American Standard Bible, © The Lockman Foundation, 1960, 1962, 1963, 1968, 1971, 1972, 1973, 1975, 1977.

CONTENTS

America! America!
God shed His grace on thee,
and crown Thy good with brotherhood
From sea to shining sea.

THE LONG VIEW

Did you ever wonder what the world would look like, if you were a hawk, if you were circling higher and higher on rising air currents in front of a massive storm?

If you were a prairie hawk, soaring above the Missouri River in April, that mighty river would look like a thin brown line running through grass that stretched to the horizon and was just turning green.

And if the year were 1843, you'd be looking down at clusters of white specks gathered by the river—the canvas covers of hundreds of pioneer wagons, getting ready to head west.

That's the fun of books: you can see these things in your mind. You take the description from the page, and using your imagination, you create the scene. Like the scenery in a play, you build the set, and you put the people in it. From then on, that scene is yours.

That's the difference between reading a book and watching TV: when you just watch, someone else has already done all the creating for you, like a mother bird who has pre–chewed the food she sticks down her babies' gullets. You may feel something as you watch, but you don't use your mind. So you don't remember what happened very long because you played no part in creating it.

When you read a story, though, each scene belongs to you. You imagined it and you'll always remember it.

This book is full of scenes you'll remember. And something else special: it's not just make–believe or entertainment (though you are going to have fun reading it)! It's real: it actually happened. It's the true story of this country's first half–century as a nation. In particular, it's about the men and women, not much different from you mom and dad, who set the pattern for how things would work. In fact, a lot of the good things we take for granted today are the result of the decisions they made, and the way they chose to live.

Their decisions and how they lived together came from what they believed in. Most of them believed in God. And because they knew He loved them, they tried to live the way He wanted them to, being obedient to Him and caring for one another—even for the ones who were sometimes difficult.

They believed that God had a plan for each one of them, and their job was to find out what it was and then ask His help in doing it. They also believed that He had a plan for all of them together—for America.

So, get ready to imagine some pretty exciting scenes in Act Two of the American Drama, which will take you up to just before the curtain draws back on Act Three (the Civil War).

You'll join the explorers Meriwether Lewis and William Clark on their expedition into the vast Louisiana Territory and stand at the ship's rail with Francis Scott Key as he looks to see if the Stars and Stripes are still waving over Fort McHenry. You'll attend the Cane Ridge Revival, the largest camp meeting ever, which saw a third of the families in Kentucky be converted to Christ! You'll man the ramparts with Old Hickory's Tennessee riflemen, as they get ready to fight the Battle of New Orleans. You'll defend the Alamo with Jim Bowie and Davey Crockett and Cross the Great Plains with a pioneer family.

You'll meet Presidents and preachers, farmers and builders, the moms and dads who did so much to make this country great—who saw God's grace and mercy stretching from sea to shining sea.

David Manuel
Peter Marshall

CHAPTER
ONE

"For I know the plans that I have for you,"
declares the LORD. (Jeremiah 29:11)

IN GOD'S PLAN

The red banner waved in the breeze high atop the ship's main mast. Sunburned sailors with scruffy beards adjusted the rigging as their strange ship approached. On the shore excited settlers darted toward the water, hoping the ship carried supplies! The English colonists at Jamestown never had enough food.

The ship's bearded captain, dressed in frayed pantaloons and a dull green jacket, ran down the gangplank. A blue velvet hat adorned the man's greasy, matted hair. Mounted on his brown leather belt was a silvery cutlass, and two rusty knives lurked inside the folds of his purple sash. "Take me to your head man," the buccaneer ordered in broken English.

Governor John Rolfe agreed to meet with the odd visitor.

The crusty sailor introduced himself. "Me name be Cap'n Jope, sir. Me ship was headed to West Indies till a storm blew us off-course. We be low on supplies now. Give us some corn and flour and two kegs of beer, eh?"

An uneasy Rolfe hesitated before answering. Something was odd about this rough character and his sea-roving crew.

"We've no money," the captain interrupted Rolfe's thoughts. "I make you trade," he said. "I got valuable cargo aboard."

"What is this 'valuable cargo'?" Rolfe asked suspiciously.

"Slaves," the captain replied. "Nineteen Africans. I trade them to you for supplies."

Governor Rolfe granted the man's request, and the first slaves set foot on the American shore. The mysterious ship cast off and disappeared into the morning mist, never to be seen again.

The strange vessel that appeared at Jamestown that early morning in 1619 was probably a pirate ship. During the 1600s, merchants from Europe sailed to Africa as part of a growing slave trade. Violent tribes there specialized in raiding tribal villages and kidnapping unsuspecting people. These captives were traded to the merchants for casks of rum. The white traders then crammed their helpless victims like packed sardines into their ships. With little food or air, many died on the voyage. Those left were sold to Spanish plantation owners growing sugar in the West Indies.

Captain Jope and his band of renegades had probably captured such a ship, stolen the slaves, and dumped them on the small British colony in Virginia. This one incident planted the deadly seed of slavery in American soil. For the next two hundred years, its shoots would gradually develop into a jungle of savagery and greed.

In the meantime, God Almighty had charted a steady course for the country and was sending His followers to mark the way. In 1620, a special group of people set sail for the New World. They were English Christians, who had fled from religious persecution in England. After living in Holland for twelve years, they looked to the other side of the Atlantic. Their trust and commitment to Christ could be lived out in the New World.

On the morning of their departure from Holland, William Bradford stood on the barge, gazing at a large, stone windmill cranking in the breeze. Field crickets chirped in the low, green fields lining the canal. Bradford clasped his wife's hand.

"Dorothy," he said, "we're embarking on an important journey. We're pilgrims making a pilgrimage for the Lord to a new world and a new life."

Months later, on November 9, 1620, the Mayflower tacked along a grassy stretch of coastline called Cape Cod, Massachusetts. Before landing, the Pilgrims signed the Mayflower Compact. This compact laid the first cornerstone in the building of America's constitutional republic. For the first time in history, a group of free men agreed to create a government, based on God's Word and founded upon the principle that all men are created equal in His sight.

Eight years later, a second, larger group of English Puritans weighed anchor for the New World, too. As their ship sped through the calm waters of the Atlantic, Governor John Winthrop prayed in his cabin. When he finished, he removed a writing box from the chart table. Dipping his quill pen into the ink bottle, the governor wrote the words pouring from his heart.

"We have entered a covenant with God," he wrote. "We have begun a great work. And we must knit ourselves together in fellowship if we are to accomplish His plan."

Winthrop entitled his paper *A Model of Christian Charity*. It unrolled the script of God's plan even further. In the New World, God was calling the Puritans to live as a community of believers, knit together by Christ's love. They would establish a Bible-based society and fulfill the Lord's two great commandments:

> You shall love the Lord your God with all your heart, and with all your soul, and with all your mind. This is the great and foremost commandment. The second is like it, You shall love your neighbor as yourself. (Matthew 22:37–39)

The Puritans would band together in love with God as well as with one another. Their covenant would produce a living example of God's Kingdom on earth. God's design for America took shape as His children listened to Him and obeyed His call.

England settled thirteen colonies along the East Coast during the late 1600s and early 1700s. Many settlers yearned for religious freedom. Others coveted a life of quick riches and wealth. But everyone wanted land, and they discovered it in rich, luscious measure. Scented pine forests throbbed with wildlife. The blue-green bays brimmed with fish and fowl. And the eastern seacoast pulsed with activity. In the North, Puritans staked out their towns and villages with faith and hard work. The rocky land turned many from soil to sea, and soon the area bristled

14

with such industries as fishing, shipbuilding, and metal-works. To the South, the Cavaliers and Huguenots carved out large plantations of tobacco, rice, and indigo in the deep red soil and gentle climate.

The Puritans built their new lives on the biblical principle that all men are equal in God's sight. To get ahead in New England, a man needed a strong back, willing heart, and quick mind. But it was different in the South. Southerners reproduced the aristocratic heritage of their European ancestors. And the South developed into a class-ordered society. Wealthy plantation owners resided at the top of the social and economic ladder. Merchants and small farmers perched in the middle while slaves squatted at the bottom. Already, the seed of slavery was rooting its way deep into southern soil.

"To arms, to arms!" the rider shouted. "The war's begun! They're heading for Concord!" Paul Revere galloped toward Lexington, Massachusetts. He slowed his horse and shouted again, then sped off to warn others.

It was early dawn on April 19, 1775.

"Stand your ground!" Captain John Parker directed. "Don't fire unless fired upon. If they want war, let it begin here!"

The early morning light shined through the shade trees on Lexington green. The sky was clear. All was quiet. Suddenly, the church bell clanged.

"Here they come!" someone cried. The men faced the east corner of the green to see the first ranks of a column of

British soldiers. The American patriots braced themselves for battle against the greatest military force on earth.

The War for Independence had begun. Later, on July 4, 1776, the colonies formally declared their independence from England in the Declaration of Independence.

> We hold these Truths to be self-evident: that all men are created equal, that they are endowed by their Creator with certain unalienable rights, that among these are life, liberty, and the pursuit of happiness . . . .
> We, therefore, the representatives of these United States of America . . . declare, that these united colonies are . . . free and independent states.

Life, liberty, and the pursuit of happiness—these were the principles that ignited the war. Over and over again, the British Parliament and King George had refused to permit the colonies to pursue their calling of life and liberty. They had restricted them from trading. They had imposed heavy taxes. They had summoned militia to enforce the burdensome laws. Patriots across the land rose up in alarm and cried treason. "No king but King Jesus!" they proclaimed. "We are left no choice but to resist this tyranny. We must stand for freedom and follow the vision of our forefathers!"

And resist they did. Was God on their side? History proves that He was. Many times during the War for Independence, sudden changes of weather helped the beleaguered American soldiers. Amazing stories of divine intervention on the battlefields demonstrated His favoring the patriots. George Washington, their "praying general," mobilized the weary Continental Army with the example of his faith. God was clearly on their side, and they would win. Freedom! Freedom!

In the 1783 Treaty of Paris that formally ended the war, the United States of America was recognized by the nations of the world as a free and independent country. It was an historic moment. God's plan to create His Kingdom on earth had taken a big step forward. Now, it was time for the thirteen states to enter into a written covenant with one another, and become one nation under God. America could now fulfill Christ's Great Commission and offer the world an example of the Covenant Way.

Delegates from the thirteen states gathered in Philadelphia. The last rays of the setting sun streamed through the tall windows of Independence Hall. The midsummer humidity of 1787 was brutal. The men slumped behind desks covered with green felt. Some tried to concentrate on the endless arguing. Others did not care. Alexander Hamilton, a delegate from New York, had already stomped home in disgust. One representative from a smaller state was standing and pleading with the other for equality.

"A national government must be based on equal representation," he raved. "If we determine representation by the population of a state, the smaller states will lose power!"

Benjamin Franklin listened as the speakers rambled on. He pulled the watch out of his waistcoat and peered through the spectacles perched on the end of his nose. *Oh my*, he thought, *still a half hour to go*. Franklin glanced toward George Washington, who was sitting at the president's table and presiding over this miserable affair. "When will all this bickering end?" he muttered to himself as he slid his watch back into his pocket.

The speaker sat down. Franklin caught Washington's eye and indicated that he wished to speak. The general nodded. The elder statesman stood up and leaned on his walking stick while he spoke.

"At the beginning of our War for Independence," Franklin began, "we had daily prayers in this room for divine protection. Our prayers were heard, and they were graciously answered. Have we now forgotten this powerful Friend? Do we think we no longer need His assistance?"

Dead silence filled the room. Franklin continued, "I have lived a long time. And the longer I live, the more I am convinced that God governs in the affairs of man. If a sparrow cannot fall without His notice, can an empire rise without His aid?

"Without the Lord, we shall fare no better than the builders of Babel. We shall be divided by our little, local interest. We shall become a reproach to future ages."

Franklin shifted his weight and concluded, "I therefore move that from now on, we begin each session in prayer, asking the assistance of heaven and its blessing on our deliberations."

Franklin sat down. No one said a word. It was clearly the most extraordinary speech anyone had delivered in the entire three months the delegates had been meeting. And it marked a turning point in the convention. They immediately declared three days of prayer and fasting, to seek God's help in breaking the deadlock among them. At the end of that time, all the resentment and wrangling were gone. At last, the delegates got down to the task of writing a constitution for the United States of America.

The representatives agreed to a federal system that divided the political authority between one national government and many state governments. Power in the national body would be balanced between three branches. The Congress, or legislative branch, would make the laws. The Supreme Court, or judicial branch, would interpret the law. And the President would lead the executive branch.

To reach this balance, the delegates compromised on a host of issues. One of the major issues focused on the question of representation. The larger states wanted population to determine the number of representatives in Congress. The smaller states disagreed. James Madison finally devised a plan. They would create two houses. The Senate would have an equal number of delegates from each state, while population would determine the number of delegates from each state in the House of Representatives.

But other problems reared their ugly heads. How should slaves be counted? Southerners argued that the national census must include blacks. Northerners disagreed. Emotions boiled as they debated the issue.

"We want slaves counted in the population," a southern gentleman declared on the floor of the chamber.

"No!" countered a northern colleague. "Slaves are property. Counting them in the census upsets the balance of power in the federal government. It will give the South an unfair advantage."

The fact that this was the hottest summer Philadelphia

had seen in a long time did not help matters. The temperature inside Independence Hall blazed. After many days, the delegates finally agreed. They would treat slaves as partial inhabitants for the census. Five black slaves would equal three white men.

But the controversy surrounding slaves raged on. What role should the national government play with regard to slavery? Should it have the power to limit slave trading? A southern representative from a large Virginia plantation stood before the packed assembly. The lace ruffles of his white linen shirt hung limply around his neck. He had already removed his tan waistcoat because of the humidity.

"The present question doesn't just concern the states alone," George Mason maintained. "It concerns the entire Union. The institution of slavery will bring the judgment of heaven on our country. It's essential that the government have the power to prevent slavery from increasing!"

Other southern representatives objected. Georgia's youngest delegate, Charles Pinckney, rose to speak. "Leave the southern states alone. They'll probably stop importing slave labor on their own."

Pinckney's older cousin, General Charles Cotesworth Pinckney, jumped to his feet, his powdered white wig damp with sweat. "You must realize one thing," he declared with his fist in the air. "Even if we agree with you, our states will never ratify a national constitution that prohibits the trading of slaves." Pounding his fist on the desk, the elder Pinckney thundered, "The mention of slavery in the Constitution will be on our terms! If not, we'll walk out!"

It was now September 1787. The convention had

dragged into its fourth month. The delegates were exhausted. They wanted harmony, but they wanted to go home. So they reached another compromise. The Constitution would mention slavery, but Congress could not regulate slave trading until 1808. Get the Union together first. Let Congress deal with slavery later.

With the signing of the Constitution, a new era dawned for the United States. But what happened to the country after the Constitution? Would God continue to weave His design for democracy into the quilt of American life? Read on and discover the answer. It lies hidden in the fascinating story of the mountain men, statesmen, and Presidents God used to shed His grace from sea to shining sea.

Atlantic Ocean

APPALACHIAN MOUNTAINS

OHIO RIVER

MISSISSIPPI

Gulf of Mexico

22

*Watch yourself, lest you forget the LORD who brought you from the
land of Egypt, out of the house of slavery. (Deuteronomy 6:12)*

HEADING WEST

It was hard for Caleb Hotchkiss even to think about leaving. Aspetuck Corners was home. Caleb knew every bend in the winding creek with the beautiful mountain laurel growing along the banks. He and his father had planted many of the white oak trees. His grandfather had built the barn and planted the wisteria now beginning to bud. He could hardly bear the thought of never seeing it again.

Yet, like many other New Englanders in 1796, Caleb yearned for a better life. The good farmland in New England was worn out from overuse. Once, four acres could support a cow. Now it took eight or ten. Yankee farmers like Caleb were working themselves to death just to stay even.

Caleb stood by the gatepost of his wooden fence and ran his hand over the smooth finish. A lot of his friends had already left. In the spring of 1795, Amos Finley had headed to Ohio with his family. Caleb missed him.

The farmer ambled up the stone path toward the two-bedroom, white clapboard house his grandfather had built so many years ago. He walked inside. He stopped at the mahogany drop-leaf table his Grandmother Hotchkiss had ordered from London. He lingered at the tall cherry cupboard he and his father had constructed during the winter of '70. He scanned the woven rug Rachel and her mother had made. When he reached the lowboy, he pulled out Amos's letter and sat down. Carefully, he smoothed the creases and read his friend's words.

> It's true. Everything we heard and couldn't believe. There are shade trees everywhere, and creeks, and gentle hills. The soil isn't red. It's black as gunpowder and so deep, you can put a shovel all the way in to the top.
>
> You'd best pack up Rachel and your young ones and get our here while there is still plenty of bottom land. Come to East Liverpool. I have 120 acres just eight miles west of the river. I put some money down on another piece the same size alongside it, to hold for you. It'll cost you $2 an acre.

Caleb stopped reading and gazed at the heavy, blue linen curtains pulled back with a tie. He noticed a robin pecking seeds outside the kitchen. He focused on the letter again.

> It took us about six weeks to get here. It shouldn't take you as long, now that they've extended the Pennsylvania Turnpike to Philadelphia. If you leave in April, you'll have time to get a corn crop planted and a cabin up before it turns cold.

24

Leave in April. The words turned over and over in Caleb's mind. He placed the letter back in the drawer. How could he leave? His grandparents had come to America from England when his father was just a boy. They had worked this land. They were buried in the churchyard. His parents were there, too. How could he leave?

A long, dry spell in April ruined Caleb's wheat crop. The discouraged farmer realized what he must do. He visited Piet Vanderpoel, his new neighbor. Vanderpoel was milking his cow in the barn. The big Dutchman straightened up and wiped his hands on his work apron.

"Ja, Herr Hotchkiss?"

"Came to see if you'd be interested in buying my land," Caleb replied, getting right to the point.

"Be you heading west, then?" Vanderpoel asked. Caleb nodded.

"Well, we'll be sorry to see you go. You've been good neighbors." The Dutchman smiled.

"I've got 36 acres," Caleb gulped. The words were not coming easily. "It's not much for growing wheat anymore, but I expect it'd still be good for grazing."

"How much be you wanting for it?"

"Well, I reckon the land is worth $15 an acre, plus $300 for the house and $100 for the barn. Throw in another $50 for the corncribs, and I'll leave the big tools for you."

Vanderpoel rubbed the red stubble on his chin. "Your fields have rocks coming through, like the top of a bald man's head," the kindly Dutchman chuckled. "But God's been good to us, and having you as neighbors has been part of that. I'll give you $1200."

Caleb's mouth fell open. "Mr. Vanderpoel, that's more than fair! I don't know what to say."

The tanned Dutchman's blue eyes sparkled. "I'll never forget how your Rachel helped us last winter, when my Tinike had the pox."

Vanderpoel extended his right hand. Caleb shook it and quickly turned away so the man would not see the tears in his eyes.

During the next few days, Caleb and Rachel had to decide what to carry on their journey. Their wagon only had so much room. Many Hotchkiss family heirlooms had to be left behind. After much discussion, they agreed to load their four-poster bed. Everything else stayed.

Caleb and his son, Aaron, distributed the load on the wagon. Caleb folded the hooked rug his grandmother had made, as a nest for his two children. Then he checked the tools. He would need the plow, the scythe, the crosscut saw, the hammer, and nails. Alongside them he placed his long rifle, the powder horn, ammunition, wadding, and extra powder. No one knew what lay ahead.

"Ready, Pa." Aaron's words cut across his father's thoughts. Caleb nodded and yelled for the others to get up on the wagon.

"No looking back now," he directed as he slapped the leather reins on Bessy's back. The team leaned into its harness, and the wheels of the heavy wagon rumbled as they started to roll. Caleb could hear Rebecca crying softly in the back. He felt the lump in his own throat and was tempted to look back, but he didn't.

They turned out the gate toward Greenfield Hill. "Bye,

Mr. Vanderpoel," Aaron shouted to the Dutchman and his wife, who were standing by the fence, waving. "Take care of Aspetuck Corners for us."

The team settled into a slow and steady pace. They could make 30 miles by nightfall. The family rode in silence. They were sad now, but time would fix that. It always did. In a couple of days, they would be thinking ahead, instead of back.

Caleb was lost in his thoughts. What was East Liverpool, Ohio like? It would be so good to grow crops in deep, rich soil. What would he plant? Potatoes right away, and oats for the team, but mostly corn, as Amos had said. Corn kept well and could be used in so many ways, like ashcakes, cornbread, and johnnycakes. Caleb's mouth watered at the thought.

The wagon approached a fork in the road. Before Caleb could twitch the reins, the horses turned right toward Fairfield. Caleb smiled. As Rachel would say, they were in God's hands. His mother used to talk that way, too. But she had died in the winter of '63. Caleb left the praying and churchgoing to Rachel. Oh, he would raise the children never to lie or cheat or steal. He would teach them to work hard and honor their word. But he would leave the things of God to others.

"Caleb," Rachel suddenly exclaimed, "look at the wagons! They must stretch all the way back to Bridgeport!"

Dozens of wagons bumped along the rocky road in front of them, stirring the dust into smoke. The Hotchkiss family waited for an opening in line. Wheels rumbled and axles creaked as the line of canvas covered wagons passed.

Fathers, dressed in loose-fitting shirts tied at the waist, cracked whips on teams of horses or yoked oxen. Mothers in colored smocks pulled their sunbonnets low to keep out the dust. Children peeked out the back at the pack horses or cows trailing behind.

It was a Great Migration. All over New England, homesteaders were packing their wagons and heading west. Some would turn north to pursue the Hudson River up to Albany. Others would ferry across the Hudson at New York City and move west through New Jersey. The Hotchkiss family was heading south toward Pittsburgh and the Ohio River.

All of the homesteaders sought land. And opportunity—lots of opportunity. And it all lay west, across the Appalachian Mountains. At the end of the War for Independence, Americans looked over their shoulders and across the mountains toward new land. The Treaty of Paris had established new geographical boundaries. The Great Lakes now framed in the northern border, with the Mississippi River to the west, and Spanish Florida to the south. Americans along the East Coast blazed paths through the uncharted wilderness that sprawled from the Appalachians to the Mississippi.

During the late 1800s, Congress passed a series of laws encouraging settlers, like Caleb, to move to the Northwest Territory. This was a vast area marked out by the Great Lakes, the Mississippi River, and the Ohio River. The Land Ordinance of 1785 divided the territory, with many acres selling for as little as one dollar. The Northwest Ordinance of 1787 laid out the area's political development. When the population of a particular area reached 60,000, the settlers could apply for statehood. Americans eventually carved the states of Ohio, Illinois, Indiana, Michigan, and Wisconsin out of this territory.

Even though Yankee pioneers flocked across the mountains, traveling was far from easy. Without roads and maps, they followed winding rivers and streams. They cleared paths through hundreds of miles of dark, deep forest, hacking at underbrush and trees. They slept under the stars. They trudged across hills and valleys. And they fought the Indians.

War parties of Indians ambushed unsuspecting pioneers steering their way along the rivers on flatboats and log rafts. They attacked settlers in lonely wagons traveling through the woods. Hooting and hollering, Indian braves scalped their victims and skinned them alive. Frequently, they burned their prisoners at the stake while laughing and dancing at their agony. The attacks were brutal.

Along the Canadian border, British forces encouraged the Indians to resist this migration of settlers into the territory. Lieutenant Governor Simcoe of Canada set up Fort Miami, a garrison at the rapids of the Maumee River near present-day Detroit. Simcoe convinced an entire armed force of Indian tribes to fight the Americans. Shawnee, Miami, and Iroquois warriors smeared streaks of paint across their brows. Ottawa, Chippewa, and Patawotomi braves tattooed their bodies. The Sauk and Fox tribes from Lake Superior polished their tomahawks and bows. The Indians in the Northwest Territory were going on the warpath. No settler in the region was safe.

In 1794, Congress appointed Major General Anthony Wayne to defend the area. If anyone could halt the uprising, "Mad Anthony" Wayne could. Wayne stationed his troops in Ohio. By the spring of 1794, they were ready.

In August, the two sides clashed near Fort Miami. The Indians hid in a field of fallen trees near the fort.

"Charge!" an American captain ordered his squadron of cavalry, and the other forces followed.

The soldiers jumped their horses over the timber and swarmed in toward the Indians. Infantry and riflemen poured out a volley of fire. Foot soldiers charged with their bayonets. The Indians barely had time to escape. The Battle of Fallen Timbers lasted only 40 minutes, but it brought an end to the Indian attacks in the Northwest Territory.

Settlers migrating west in the late 1700s shared a common dream. They wanted to achieve a better standard of living. These Yankee pioneers, raised in the Puritan tradition of hard work, believed they could reach this goal. And they soon gained quite a reputation for their resourceful ways.

In 1798, the Reverend Benjamin Mortimer recorded a story told to him by an innkeeper along the Great Pittsburgh Road. It was the story of Stone Soup and it is often told to illustrate Yankee cleverness.

A family from Connecticut was traveling west. Before reaching their destination, they ran out of money and supplies. With a sick child, the parents became desperate to find food.

One morning, the pioneers passed a log house.

"Look, they have a vegetable garden," the wife remarked as they neared the dwelling. The family paused to admire the tomatoes and cabbages. They drooled as they eyed the lettuce and the squash. The parents decided to stop and ask for help. The father knocked on the side door. It opened instantly.

"Off with you!" a woman screamed as she waved her flour-covered hands in the air. "I'll have none of you. I'm not running an inn here, you know." The woman wiped her hands on a white apron with large pockets in the front. "I've had entirely too many of your sort knocking at my door for a free handout. Shoo!"

The surprised husband quickly withdrew. He and his wife talked a few minutes. Then the wife walked over to the kitchen window.

"Madam, may I borrow a kettle to make my sick child some stone soup?" the Yankee wife cleverly asked, as she peeked in the window.

The woman of the house looked up from her cutting board.

"Stone soup?" she inquired with a puzzled expression on her face. "You must be joking. I've never heard of such a thing."

"Oh, yes," the mother replied. "It's exceedingly delicious. And it's just the thing for someone getting over a fever."

Hmmm, the woman thought. *I wonder if this soup could help my sickly husband?* She put down her cutting knife and opened the door. "Why don't you come in?"

"It's not difficult to make," the traveling wife explained as the woman retrieved a kettle to place over the fire. "I'll show you how so you can do it yourself." The woman agreed, and the two women began.

"First, you need a large flat, smooth stone from a neighboring brook," the traveler explained.

"I have one right here, near the fireplace. It should do, don't you think?"

"Yes, it'll do nicely," the traveler answered. She placed it in the bottom of the kettle over the fire with plenty of water and a little salt.

As the water boiled, the traveler took a sip. "I think it could use some turnips and perhaps some carrots. Potatoes would improve the taste, too."

The woman of the house cheerfully provided the vegetables. Soon the mother tasted the soup again. She nodded. "It's getting better. But it would be first rate if it had some meat in it."

No sooner had she said this than the housewife produced a shinbone of beef. "Here you are," she smiled with a gleam in her eye, placing the beef into the soup.

The kettle simmered for a long while. The two women added spices to improve the flavor.

"I believe it's ready," the traveling wife announced.

Just then, the man of the house walked into the kitchen. He had white hair and a beard. His skin looked like brown leather from having worked in the sun.

"What smells so good?" he asked as he approached the hearth.

"It's called stone soup, Pa," his wife answered. "We've just made it."

"Well, let's have some!" the old man suggested.

And so, the man, his wife, and the traveling family sat down to a delicious meal of stone soup.

"Ma, this is the best thing I've ever put in my mouth!" Pa exclaimed. "You must get the recipe."

And the woman did.

> Take a large, flat, smooth stone from a spring. Put it into a pot with water and vegetables to suit your taste. Add a bone of meat. Flavor to your liking. Boil for several hours. Note: the same stone can be used a number of times, but it must be kept clean.

Americans up and down the East Coast blazed paths across the mountains toward the Mississippi. Pioneers from as far north as Massachusetts and as far south as Georgia glutted the routes west. By 1796, 100,000 Virginians had moved into Kentucky, Tennessee, and Ohio.

Unfortunately, however, this migration over the mountains differed from the earlier pilgrimage across the Atlantic Ocean. Unlike their forefathers, these newcomers had set the things of God aside. Like Caleb, many of them carried a strong sense of right and wrong. But they no longer sought God's guidance nor placed Him at the center of their lives. They thought they had more important things to do, like plow new land and build new homes. While churches still provided places of worship, especially in the Puritan north, preachers no longer led the flocks. America was forgetting God.

In many ways, this Great Migration was not so great at all. Without God's guidance, America could miss its divine mission. How would God bring these wayward pioneers back into dependence on Him? How would He remind them of the covenant commitment He had made with their forefathers? As we will soon discover, He sent a special group of Christian scouts committed to spreading His light across the West.

CHAPTER
THREE

Revive me according to Thy loving-kindness,
So that I may keep the testimony of Thy mouth. (Psalms 119:88)

REVIVAL

One bright, sunny day, an engineer from Kentucky was swimming with a survey party in the St. John's River in Florida. Out of nowhere, an alligator suddenly grabbed the engineer and dragged him under the water. Before long, the two rose to the surface. The reptile looked like a large green lizard with eyes sticking out above its skull. Its long, scaly tail thrashed about in the water, splashing everything. Sharp teeth gripped the victim's right leg in a powerful jaw, twisting and turning to break the leg off. The alligator's smooth, tan belly flipped over in the water. The other engineers watched in stunned amazement.

"Help him!" an officer in a nearby boat screamed.

"No!" the Kentuckian shot back. "Give the fellow a fair play!"

The engineer then thrust one of his thumbs through his captor's eye socket. The astounded reptile unclinched its jaw and released the man's leg. As the alligator paddled away, the triumphant Kentuckian swam toward shore. The

35

men shouted for joy. Yep, those Kentuckians could beat just about anything!

"There's no place on the universal earth like old Kaintuck," an old boatman on the Ohio River once said. And many people at that time thought he was right. As settlers threaded their way through the mountains in the late 1700s, many headed toward Kentucky. Trudging through the Cumberland Gap, cut by Daniel Boone, the pioneers passed by redbuds and mountain magnolias decorating the Appalachian Plateau. They crossed grasslands filled with roaming buffalo and elk. A spirit of adventure filled their hearts.

Men in buckskin cleared the land, chopping trees and plowing between the stumps. They built log cabins by the sweat of their brow. They learned to survive on salt pork and hard liquor. And they boasted about everything they did. Proud and boisterous, the Kentucky pioneers soon developed a reputation for their sharpshooting and their rabble-rousing. Nothing stopped them. No rules governed them. Losing an eye or an ear in a fight branded them as courageous.

Technically, United States law governed Kentucky in 1796. But no one enforced it. Without law enforcement officers, outlaws combed the land, doing as they pleased. One particular county attracted so many murderers, horse thieves, and robbers that it was nicknamed "Rogues Harbor".

One day, a Presbyterian minister named James McGready rode into Rogues Harbor. Wearing the buckskin breeches of his fellow Kentuckians, McGready preached the Gospel. He spoke simply and easily, describing the glories of heaven and the horrors of hell. His humble attitude and his honesty touched the hearts of the townspeople in Rogues Harbor. In 1797, three small congregations sprang up, located on three rivers in the county, the Muddy River, the Red River, and the Gasper River.

McGready covenanted with his churches to pray for revival. They asked God to awaken people's interest in Him. In July 1799, a small revival broke out at Red River. The next month, another one kindled the Gasper River congregation. The news traveled fast. In 1800, more than 500 people attended a quarterly communion service at the Red River church. And here, McGready received the answer to his prayers.

During the final service on Sunday evening, a visiting Methodist minister, named John McGee, was preaching. He described what happened.

> I was encouraging the congregation to let the Lord reign in their hearts and submit to Him. Many broke silence . . . the power of God was strong upon me . . . I went through the house exhorting with all possible ecstasy and energy.

Salvation swept through the assembly hall that night. And word about this spread across the territory, attracting lost, lonely frontier families like a giant magnet. Folks headed for a July meeting at Gasper River.

"Let's cut a clearing over there," McGready directed, pointing to a section in the woods. "The preachers can speak from the platforms we build. We'll split logs for the benches."

The church members worked for days building the campgrounds, but no one expected what happened. Ten thousand people showed up! Traveling in wagons, on horseback, and by foot, people from all over the state arrived to experience the reality of God's Holy Spirit.

McGready surveyed the scene. White, wispy clouds adorned a blue sky. A bright Kentucky sun cast shadows through the hardwood trees. Loaded supply wagons circled the camp's perimeter while tents and lean-tos dotted the clearing. The pastor studied the people. Groups of spectators walked around the camp, listening to the preachers. Some folks knelt on the ground, lifting their hearts and hands toward heaven. Others sang melodies or praise and worship. "No one wanted to go home," McGready wrote. "Hunger and sleep did not matter. Eternal things were the main concern."

After that meeting at Gasper River, camp meetings sprang up all across Kentucky. In 1801, Reverend Barton Stone and his Cane Ridge congregation planned a summer revival. Little did they realize what was about to take place.

Hundreds of wagons choked the approach roads to Cane Ridge during the week before the meeting. Dust coated everything in their path. Fathers wearing straw hats drove the teams, while mothers and children sat on top of covered supplies. Some people rode horses while others walked. The first arrivals helped clear the space and construct the preaching platforms.

Twenty-five thousand people showed up for the Cane Ridge revival. Rifle-toting rogues and greasy backwoods men appeared, hungry for God's Word. Families gathered together to listen to the preaching. And God's Holy Spirit moved among them all. Pastors led hundreds in the salvation prayer at one time. "Lord Jesus Christ, Son of God, I confess that I am a sinner, and I ask You now to forgive me for all my sins. I accept your forgiveness, Lord, and I invite You to come into my heart. I give my life to You now, and from now on, You will be my Lord and Master. Amen." People fell to the ground, slain in the power of the Holy Spirit. Folks raised their hands in adoration and praise. Great numbers shouted at once, like the roar of Niagara Falls.

As this meeting at Cane Ridge ended, waves of revival flooded the west. They rushed across the mountain gaps, over the rough turnpikes, and down the surging rivers. God had not forgotten His covenant with His people. He had not forsaken His vision for America. And through the boisterous thunder of revivalist preachers, He was reminding them of His great love.

Before long, an advance troop of Christian soldiers dispersed to evangelize the west. They traveled on horseback, holding meetings and preaching the gospel. Because each of them was responsible for his own circular route, they were called circuit riders. One of the most famous was a Methodist preacher named Francis Asbury.

One cold November evening, Asbury trotted down a muddy, dirt road. Pulling his cloak around him, he patted the neck of his nervous gray mare. She shivered beneath him from the sleet and rain.

"We'll get there, old girl," he promised. "You'll have your oats before nightfall."

Asbury glanced up at the darkening sky and tried not to worry. *Father,* he prayed, *please take care of Jane tonight. She's such a faithful horse.* The preacher tilted his head so the brim of his black hat would keep the rain from his blue eyes. *And me as well, Lord,* he quickly added. *Please watch over me this night.*

The evangelist and his horse had traveled many miles together. This year, they had trotted through Virginia and the Carolinas. They had crossed the Appalachians into Kentucky and Tennessee. This past week, they had covered over 200 miles to reach people for Jesus.

"Thank You, Lord, that Your grace is sufficient wherever I may be," the cold rider whispered.

Suddenly, a large swollen stream cut across their path. Rushing waters swirled in front of them. Jane cautiously started to cross, but her hooves sank in the deep mud, and icy water surged about her forelegs. Deeper and deeper they went. Soon, water covered the rider's feet, filling his boots and soaking his last pair of dry socks. The mare stumbled. For an instant, it looked as if they would both be swimming for their lives.

"You can do it, girl!" Asbury shouted over the noisy wind and rain. "God is with us, Jane. We still have work to do. We're going to make it across!"

At once, the mare regained her footing and clambered up the other bank. Shaking her wet mane, she gave a low, gentle neigh. Yes, they still had work to do.

"Good girl," Asbury exclaimed. "We've only a few miles to go now. The Whitley family will take us in tonight. Remember them? They accepted Jesus last summer."

Francis Asbury broke out in song. This was his life, riding circuit and preaching Christ to anyone and everyone who would listen. This was his life, reaching lost Americans who did not know Jesus.

In 1771, Francis Asbury had come to America from England to preach. And his preaching inspired all who listened. A typical year of travel included Massachusetts, Connecticut, New York, Pennsylvania, Maryland, Virginia, the Carolinas, Kentucky, and Tennessee. Some years, he rode 4,000 miles on horseback, spreading the Gospel and bringing people to salvation.

Asbury traveled constantly, and he loved to preach. Although he kept busy, he always had time for Bible reading and prayer. He could recite long passages of Scripture by heart, including the New Testament. He cared for the lost, and he loved God's people. Gradually, easterners and westerners alike came to recognize the commanding figure with blue eyes, white hair, and black cloak. As one man described him, "There was such a dignity about him. He seemed to be born to sway others."

Another famous saddlebag evangelist who rode for Jesus was Peter Cartwright. A big, two-fisted preacher, Cartwright had first met Jesus during a camp meeting run by James McGready. His messy hair, piercing black eyes, and two-hundred-pound frame commanded everyone's attention. When Cartwright bellowed forth a sermon in his booming voice, everyone listened, even the rogues.

One night, Cartwright was traveling through the Cumberland Mountains and decided to stop at a particular inn. That evening, the inn held a dance. People from miles around attended.

The evangelist sat at a wood table on the sidelines, watching the merrymakers. A young woman with jet black hair approached his table. She looked striking in her white petticoat, deerskin smock, and tan moccasins.

"Would you care to dance, sir?" the woman asked.

Cartwright stood up, bowed at the waist and escorted her to the middle of the dance floor. The fiddler lifted his bow for the next dance. But the preacher raised his right hand. The hall grew still.

"For years, I've never taken a step without asking the Lord's blessing," he said in his deep voice. "I'd like to ask God's blessing on this beautiful young woman and on all of you, who've been so kind."

Cartwright fell to his knees. "Oh, Lord," he prayed, "bless this company with Thy presence. Show them their sinful ways. Take them into Thy arms, Father, and show them Your mercy."

The bang of a falling chair pierced the quiet. A few guests fled from the hall, but many others remained. Some wept. Some fell to their knees.

The evangelist stood up. "You must turn from your wicked ways!" he shouted. "God loves you. He has a plan for your life. He sent His Son Jesus to die on a cross for you." Cartwright's voice rose with emotion. "Turn your life over to Him."

The evangelist then rattled the windows with a hymn of

praise. The young woman at his side cried out to God for mercy. Folks started weeping. By the time the night was over, many had given their lives to Christ.

Men like Francis Asbury and Peter Cartwright moved like needles of light across the west, quilting regions together with the common thread of a shared faith in Christ. They brought thousands to repentance and salvation, and they helped turn people's hearts back to God. As the sun rose on the nineteenth century, God did not want His people to forget their covenant with Him. He was calling the western frontiersmen back to Himself.

But what was happening to the people back east? Had God forgotten them?

CHAPTER
FOUR

See to it that no one takes you captive through philosophy and empty deception, . . . according to the elementary principles of the world, rather than according to Christ. (Colossians 2:8)

THE SECOND GREAT AWAKENING

Lyman Beecher ran toward the commons and jumped the wood fence surrounding the green. He dashed across the grass, passing a number of students walking to class.

Yale College is so beautiful in the spring, Lyman thought as he hurried along the cobblestone path, past the red brick buildings. *I'm glad God permitted me to come here. So many ideas, so many new things to do.*

Lyman resembled the other undergraduates strolling about campus. He wore a navy blue frock coat and breeches. His light stockings contrasted with his black buckle shoes. The ruffles of his white shirt flapped in the breeze as he ran. But he did not wear a red, knitted cap like the many Jacobins who attended Yale. Lyman was not a member of their French revolutionary society, although he had heard tales about their wild parties and their heated debates.

Gripping his books tightly, Lyman scurried toward Connecticut Hall. *I'd best not be late,* he thought. *President*

Dwight will have started, and I don't want to miss any of the discussion today.

The panting student arrived at Connecticut Hall, a modest, two-story, brick building. With its white trimmed windows, the distinguished building reflected the colonial architecture of the times. Lyman heard robins chirping in the elm trees nearby as he opened the door.

Yale's campus bristled with activity on this spring day in 1798. Since its founding in 1701, the college had trained many men for the ministry. By 1798, however, things were changing. Hardly anyone was studying to be a minister anymore. Few students attended the college church, and only two professors in the entire school taught religion. But Dr. Timothy Dwight wanted to change this. Since becoming president in 1795, Dwight had been trying to steer the college back toward its religious purpose. To do this, Dwight held frank, open discussions with the students. Lyman Beecher was hurrying to one of these meetings now.

Beecher pulled open the heavy door and walked inside. Wooden boards creaked under his shoes. In the lecture hall, students sat on benches in front of a podium. Lyman quietly slipped inside. The meeting had just begun.

"Sir," one student was saying, "it seems to me that the point of view coming out of France is quite reasonable. We should use our minds to think things through. By doing this, we'll discover truth. God has nothing to do with it."

Clasping his hands together, Dr. Dwight leaned against the lectern. "It's important to develop a well-trained and disciplined mind," he responded. "Our Puritan heritage teaches us that. But we must place this tool at the feet of

God to be used for His glory. Otherwise, we'll be at the mercy of our own sinful nature."

Another student raised his hand. The president acknowledged him. "Yes, Mr. Stuart?"

"Sir, the people in France revolted a few years ago because they wanted a democratic republic like ours." Mr. Stuart rose to his feet as he spoke. "They overthrew King Louis XVI and set up a national assembly. Now, we're receiving terrible reports about mob violence and beheadings over there. What's going wrong?"

Dwight scratched his chin for a moment and straightened his waistcoat. Lyman was struck by how dignified and impressive he looked.

"Your question is a good one," the president replied. "It's a noble goal to want democratic freedom. We fought long and hard against the tyranny of Great Britain to achieve ours. But we had something the French don't have. We had faith in God. We asked for Divine guidance. General Washington prayed constantly, and God honored those prayers.

"The French don't have this spiritual background. Their revolution isn't based on the Word of God. It's grounded in their own self-interest, and it will fail."

Dwight walked over to a nearby table and leaned against it, crossing his feet and folding his arms over his chest. He went on. "Scripture is the best correction for the evil we find in society. We must look to it as our guide. The Bible directs us to respect freedom. It teaches us to submit to the authority of law and order. All men are equal in the sight of God, and they deserve equal treatment under the law. When King George and Parliament abused their authority over us, we had no choice but to resist. But our goal was not self-interest. It was to return to the Covenant Way of our forefathers. We wanted to live our lives the way God teaches in His Word.

"This isn't the case in France. The fighting in France is based on the common man's desire to have what the rich and wealthy have. They want to glorify themselves, not God. This is nothing more than selfishness and pride. And it's sin. God isn't going to bless their efforts unless they turn to Him"

President Dwight placed one hand in the side pocket of his beige breeches. "Gentlemen," he said, "this takes us to the heart of my concern for America today. The sort of thinking coming out of France is the spirit of the infidel. It's rebellion against God and His Holy Word. These Frenchmen don't believe in the God of the Bible. And we must be very careful not to adopt their way of thinking."

Lyman glanced around the room as Dwight spoke. Many of the French Jacobin students sat in the room. Beecher realized that this president was battling the rising tide of anti-Christian thought on campus. He admired him for doing this. It wasn't easy.

"But sir," a student wearing the distinctive red cap objected, "the Scriptures are outdated. This is the Age of Enlightenment. No modern man holds to the old biblical ideas about sin and a Savior. The Deists are right. We can use our minds to reason out truth."

Dwight smiled and shook his head. "Deism requires us to reject God's Word, the Bible. We must not do this. God

Himself established the moral order. Whether we like it or not, we must obey it. The Deists want us to live in a world without absolutes. They tell us God sits up in heaven and doesn't care. But this isn't true. The Bible proves that He does care.

"Let's think together for a moment. How can we run a society without God? It would be like sailing on the seas at night without a compass. How do we discover we're off course? Without an instrument or the stars to guide us, we don't. God's Word is like a compass. We need it to keep us on course as a society. Without it, what's to stop us from believing it's alright to steal or lie or even murder? Nothing. Without God, there's nothing to stop man's sinful nature from taking control."

Dwight picked up an earthenware pitcher from the table to pour himself a cup of water. After taking a sip, he continued. "Christ promised us life and life abundantly. But we must follow Him. Gentlemen of Yale, what does it profit us to gain the whole world if we lose our own souls? Scripture teaches that all have sinned and fall short of the glory of God. We cannot escape our sinful nature by thinking up arguments against it. We may debate it, but the Bible clearly states that it still exists. The only means of escape is through Jesus."

The president's words flowed clearly and easily. "Gentlemen, will you really teach your children that death is an eternal sleep? Will you tell God on Judgment Day that you didn't need Him because you reasoned Him out of existence?"

Lyman Beecher leaned forward. Not a sound could be

heard in the lecture hall except the chirping of birds outside the window. His heart pounded within his chest. Somehow the young man was hearing words that touched his heart.

Dwight's voice grew stronger. "Are you willing to live your lives on the chance there's no heaven? Are you willing to take the chance that there's no hell? Oh, to realize the depth of Christ's love for you! It brings such joy. It brings such peace. I pray that each of you will one day come to know Him as your Lord and Savior!"

The chimes of the clock rang and class was over. The young Yale men began to file out the door, but they were silent. Their hearts had been touched

Around the turn of the century, new ideas from Europe swept across the New England countryside. Europe had entered the Age of Reason, a period in which man worshipped his own ability to reason. Such philosophies as Rationalism and Deism convinced many people, especially the French, that man could answer all the questions of life. He could reason things through on his own. Man did not need God. Only ignorant and superstitious people still believed the old-fashioned ideas about sin and a Savior.

But once again, God Almighty stepped in to preserve His divine plan.

The revival in New England did not travel through thunderous preachers or great camp meetings as it had in the west. God meets people exactly where they are. New Englanders needed a gentle push, so the Almighty sent

Timothy Dwight to nudge them with love, wisdom, and kindness.

By 1802, Dwight's efforts paid off. In March, the first student at Yale confessed faith in Christ. A second student stepped forward in April. By June, many of the seniors had committed their lives. Young men, such as Lyman Beecher, began choosing the ministry as their life's work.

And the revival fanned out from the campus. One town after another turned back to God. Church members would sit in their pews one week, stifling yawns and trying not to fall asleep. The next Sunday, they would explode with praises and adoration for God. Even the ministers were amazed and excited by the change. "We have heard . . . the glad tidings of the outpourings of the Spirit," the General Assembly of the Presbyterian Church wrote. "From the east, from the west, and from the south, these joyful tidings have reached our ears."

The Holy Spirit was at work. New Englanders flocked back to church. They renewed their commitment to love God and their neighbors as themselves. They returned to the covenant life of their forefathers. Their zeal ushered in a new emphasis on missions. It motivated them to establish orphanages and hospitals, and to set up schools for the blind. People organized Bible societies and distributed Bible tracts for the first time. This change of heart also prompted the first missions trip to India in 1812. God's plan for America had endured. She was now reaching out with His love to a hurting world.

In addition to Timothy Dwight, God raised up a second general to lead His spiritual army in the early 1800s. He was Lyman Beecher.

Clang! Clang!

"Mother! The church bell is ringing," Harriet yelled as she skipped down the wooden stairs. Her blond hair was tied back with blue ribbons to match her blue stockings. Dainty, pink flowers dotted her cotton dress and blue petticoat. The young girl bounded into the hallway and almost collided with her mother, who stood at the mirror tying the ribbon on her Sunday bonnet.

"He will most certainly be late," her mother announced. "Henry, run upstairs and see if your father is ready."

Instantly, Harriet's brother Henry bounded up the stairs to their father's study. *Another typical Sunday*, he thought.

"Father!" Henry exclaimed. "It's time for Sunday service. Mother says we must be going."

Inside the study, Dr. Beecher gathered his notes and stood up. "Yes, yes," he answered, "tell your mother I'm coming. Now, let me see, perhaps I should add a point about vowing to stay away from alcohol," he mumbled. "Yes, I'll do that." The preacher sank back into his chair to make a note of the idea.

Meanwhile, the bell sounded again. "Girls, run upstairs and fetch your father. Tell him he's going to miss his own sermon if he doesn't hurry up." Mother gathered her eleven other children at the front door as she spoke. "Tell him we're at the door."

Harriet and her sister, Catherine, grabbed the wooden bannister and darted upstairs. "Father," Catherine cried through the door. "Mother says you're going to miss your own sermon! That was the last bell!"

Instantly, the door opened. A tall, angular man with

dark hair and sparkling eyes charged out of the study. "Catherine, have you seen my hat and gloves? I seem to have misplaced them."

"Mother has them downstairs," Catherine replied.

"Well and good," he said as he quickly followed them downstairs. "Harriet, please run back and fetch a pin to fasten these papers. You'll find one on my desk in the study."

Harriet obeyed, while their mother hurriedly straightened the white collar bands of her husband's shirt. "Don't forget this," she said as she handed him his black top hat.

"Let's go," he announced. With that, the family of Dr. Lyman Beecher went out the door and headed toward their father's church.

In 1826, Beecher had accepted the pulpit of the Hanover Street Congregational Church in Boston. Like the rest of New England, Boston had changed greatly since the time of the Puritans. In Boston, a belief system called Unitarianism had crept into the Church. Unitarians did not believe Christ was the Son of God, and they rejected the Trinity. They taught that human nature is not sinful and that man can become better on his own without God's help. By the time Beecher arrived, the city presented a fortress of Unitarian thought.

Dr. Beecher realized that God had placed him there for a reason. He also realized that nothing was impossible with God. With guidance from the Holy Spirit, the preacher quietly began his work.

"From the beginning," he wrote, "folks who were interested in my preaching came to listen. I kept watch and ministered privately when asked. I knew this was God's way of bringing revival to the church. I did not attack the Unitarians. I simply waited and prayed."

Gradually Beecher noticed new faces at Sunday morning services. Before long, people packed the church. Beecher started holding services in the evening. He invited the parishioners to attend meetings to explore the meaning of Christianity. Soon, 300 people were coming.

To signal these evening gatherings, Beecher rang his church bell. The Unitarian ministers did not like this one bit. Their people were attending the gatherings at Beecher's church.

"I used to laugh to hear the bells," Beecher wrote. "For a while, our church's bell was the only one ringing in the evening. Soon, Unitarian bells were clanging everywhere!"

The results of the Second Great Awakening were clearly seen in Christians of all denominations. Throughout New England they began to put the second great commandment to work as they rediscovered the importance of loving their neighbors. They established orphanages and old people's homes, hospitals, and societies to fight alcoholism. They distributed Bibles, started Sunday schools, and supported missionaries. In New Haven, Connecticut, Thomas Gallaudet met with other ministers to pray and make plans for starting the Connecticut Asylum for the Deaf and Dumb.

God was uniting His people once again. Just as He had done before the War for Independence, God's Holy Spirit was sounding His call across the rugged lands in the west and the rocky eastern coastline. Such servants as Francis Asbury, Peter Cartwright, Timothy Dwight, and Lyman Beecher heeded this call and proclaimed His kingdom.

And once again, God's timing was perfect. Very soon, the young republic would need the strength of union. Another war with Great Britain lurked around the corner. America would need faith in Christ and the help of God.

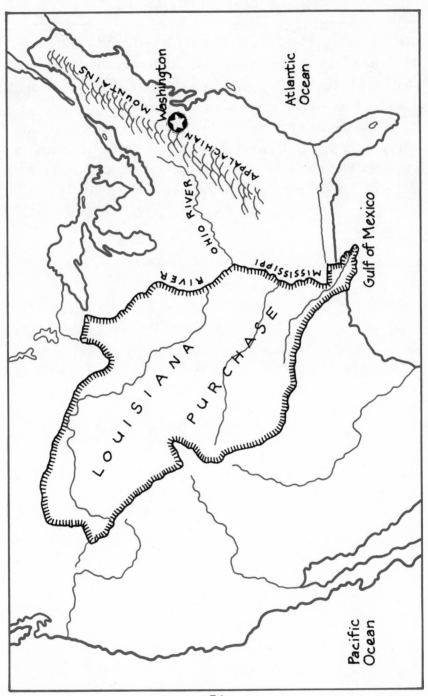

CHAPTER
FIVE

May he also rule from sea to sea. (Psalm 72:8)

THE LOUISIANA PURCHASE

Seated in his elegant carriage, Secretary of State James Madison sped down Pennsylvania Avenue from the Capitol to the White House. He clutched the papers on his lap as he gazed out the side window. Some ladies were strolling under the maple trees bordering the quiet, dirt road. A youngster and his black dog frolicked in front of one of the red brick, colonial buildings. A rider trotted by on his horse and tipped his hat.

Washington blossoms with an early spring, thought Madison. *The government moved here from Philadelphia only three years ago, and so much has happened.*

The buggy jolted down the avenue, swaying to and fro like a determined cat getting ready to pounce on its prey. Madison listened to the clip-clop of the horse's hooves and leaned back against the blue velvet cushions. He sighed. Something was up. He could feel it in his bones. He would find out as soon as he saw the President.

The Secretary of State arrived at the White House. It was

a simple but stately mansion. The second President, John Adams, and his wife had been the first to occupy the new building in 1800. Thomas Jefferson, the third President, now lived there. Mr. Madison stepped out of the carriage to enter the mansion's north side.

James Madison and Thomas Jefferson had been friends a long time. As delegates from Virginia, they had both helped write the Declaration of Independence. Madison had represented Virginia during the Constitutional Convention in 1787 while Jefferson served as ambassador to France. When Washington appointed Jefferson his Secretary of State, James Madison was elected to the U.S. House of Representatives. Jefferson selected his friend as Secretary of State after winning the election in 1801.

It was now the spring of 1803. The President waited in the map room of the White House for Mr. Madison. He sat at a large mahogany desk, drumming his fingers in rhythm. He was deep in thought.

Napoleon Bonaparte is up to something, Jefferson reflected as he looked out the window behind him. Since Spain had transferred Louisiana to France, Napoleon had refused Jefferson's negotiations to buy West Florida. But the United States had to have access to the port of New Orleans on the Mississippi. Merchants from Kentucky, western Pennsylvania, and the Ohio Valley needed to trade down the Mississippi. Without the right to deposit their goods along the coast, all trade would stop.

Jefferson glanced at the colorful sky, taking a moment to enjoy the gray and purple colors of the setting sun. An evening mist gently rolled in from the Potomac River and stayed near the ground.

Madison should be here soon, Jefferson mused. *I wonder what Bonaparte will propose. He wants Europe, and that means he faces war with England. England may try to seize his holdings in the New World. If so, she'll probably snatch New Orleans or plunge down from Canada into the Louisiana Territory. Bonaparte will need his forces here as well as in Europe. I wonder what—*

Just then, an aide knocked on the door. "Mr. President, Secretary of State Madison is here to see you."

"Ah, yes," the President replied, "show him in."

The tall, gray-haired Virginian rose from his chair to greet his visitor. As Madison entered, the President walked around the table to greet him.

"Mr. Madison," he said warmly. "It's always good to see you."

"Thank you, sir," Madison replied. "I have something here you need to see." The Secretary pulled a letter out of the papers he was carrying and handed it to Jefferson. Jefferson took a moment to read it.

"This *is* something," the President responded excitedly as he finished. "Let's take a look at the map."

The two statesmen stood at the map table. Jefferson's aid weighted down the corners of the map with silver candlesticks. In the soft glow of their light, the men stared in disbelief at the map.

"Sir, this is unbelievable," Madison exclaimed. "Napoleon wants to sell us the entire Louisiana Territory! That includes all of this!" Madison outlined with his finger the territory west of the Mississippi River. It stretched all the way from the Rocky Mountains to the edge of the Spanish territory known as Texas.

"I see now what Napoleon is up to," Jefferson remarked. "He's anticipating a move by the British in Europe. If this happens, he expects they'll try to seize French holdings in America, too. Napoleon is smart. He doesn't want Britain to get the territory under any circumstances. He also doesn't want us to set up an alliance with Britain against him. He'd rather see the United States have Louisiana, so he's going to sell to us before anything else happens."

Jefferson traced the borders of the territory in question with his fingers and shook his head. "Mr. Madison, if we act quickly, we can pull off a coup like no other in the history of the New World."

"Yes, we could," Madison agreed. "But Mr. President, the Federalist Party in Congress is going to oppose you on this. Such a decision might make you appear to favor a strong, central government that would make decisions like this. Yet, you don't."

Jefferson paused to think. A furrow wrinkled his brow. "Political parties are strange animals, James. Ever since we wrote our Constitution, people have disagreed about how much power our national government should have. And most of the time I want to see it limited. But this is an opportunity we can't refuse. Bonaparte is offering to sell us the entire parcel for $22,000,000. And this includes New Orleans. With the stroke of a pen, we can almost double the size of the United States!"

Madison looked down at the map. "But the majority of Americans trade with Europe, Mr. President. How will they feel when they discover their government is now looking toward the west, instead of back to Europe?"

"The British will grab New Orleans if they think they can get away with it. You and I both know that. We must take it while we can. We have no other choice. There are enough men of vision in Congress to see that.

"Authorize Mr. Monroe in France to negotiate an agreement with Bonaparte. We'll purchase the territory for $15,000,000."

"Yes, sir," Madison replied.

God's ways are often hidden from man. This time, He chose an American leader, who did not know His Son, to further His purpose. God Himself opened the door for Thomas Jefferson to acquire the enormous parcel of property known as the Louisiana Territory. And the United States advanced one step closer to stretching from the Atlantic to the Pacific.

Following the purchase, Jefferson assembled a group of men to explore the new territory. He asked his personal secretary, Meriwether Lewis, to head the expedition.

The twenty-six-year-old Lewis stood before his Commander in Chief. Mr. Jefferson sat at his massive oak desk, covered with maps and quill pens. "Lewis, you served under Anthony Wayne at the Battle of Fallen Timbers. I believe you're the man for this job."

Lewis listened attentively as the President spoke. His eyes squinted from the glare of the sun's rays beaming through the window behind Mr. Jefferson's chair. He could hardly contain himself. He had been pestering the President for this chance ever since learning the expedition was being planned.

"Mr. President," Lewis replied, "I'd like to request that William Clark share the command with me. He's a fellow officer and good friend of mine. You remember his brother, Colonel George Rogers Clark, the most famous Continental Army commander on the northwest frontier."

"Yes, I remember. That'll be most satisfactory."

The President dipped his quill pen into the ink bottle and drew an outline on one of the maps. "This is a scientific expedition," he explained. "I believe we can transport goods overland between the Atlantic and the Pacific. I want you to travel up the Missouri, cross the Rocky Mountains, and follow the Columbia River. That route will take you into the unclaimed Oregon Territory. Record everything you see, sending back samples of the plant and animal life.

"I'm also interested in the Indian tribes living out there. Establish communication with them. Treat them with respect, and acquaint them with our desire to be neighborly."

"Yes, sir," Lewis responded with a salute, as he turned on his heels to leave.

The sun had barely risen on the morning of May 14, 1804. Forty-three men crossed the Mississippi River at St. Louis and began their journey up the Missouri. They launched several small boats and one 55-foot keelboat. The keelboat was a large, flat-bottomed boat the men could both row and pole. The corps carried supplies for themselves as well as colored beads and trinkets for the Indians. High hopes fizzed through their minds like a bubbling soda.

The Lewis and Clark Expedition navigated its way against the slow, treacherous current of the muddy river. Sometimes the group only traveled three or four miles a day. The men passed the swampy marshlands in Missouri and the rolling plateaus of Nebraska. They coursed along the sandy plains in the Dakotas, mapping the river and checking the temperature and soil. They cataloged every plant and animal, and they recorded their experiences with the natives.

In September, the expedition encountered Indians for the first time as it journeyed through the Dakotas. About 50 Sioux shadowed them along the riverbank. These northern plains Indians hunted buffalo in the future state of Nebraska and the western Dakotas.

Landing a small boat on shore, the Americans invited the Sioux onto the keelboat and presented the chiefs with gifts of beads and trinkets. All went well, until they offered the Indians whiskey. The chiefs gulped the brew down and grabbed the bottle, passing it among themselves until it was empty. Then they demanded more.

"Tell Black Buffalo and his chiefs they must get into the small boat first," Clark instructed his interpreter. "We're going to row them back to shore."

The chiefs obliged and piled into the boat. But as soon as the craft reached shore, three Sioux braves seized the towline. The Americans were trapped.

"You cannot leave!" ordered one of the chiefs. "We want more presents!"

"We're not squaws! We're warriors!" Clark angrily shot back. "And we've been sent by our great white Father, who could exterminate you!"

"I have warriors, too!" the chief bellowed.

Immediately, Clark unsheathed his sword. On the keelboat, American fingers touched triggers. On shore, a circle of Indians put arrows to bowstrings. Sioux braves encircled Clark, and 12 Americans instantly swarmed into a small boat to aid their captain.

For a moment, all history seemed to hold its breath. But not for long. Suddenly, Black Buffalo raised his hand high in the air. The Sioux braves pulled back. Apparently, the chief had decided to stop the encounter before it got any worse. When Clark realized this, he extended his right hand in a show of friendship. Black Buffalo turned to walk away, then he turned back again.

"May we come back onto your boat?" he asked Clark.

An amazed Clark gasped silently and then replied, "Why, yes, chief, we'd be delighted."

It was a miracle. The Americans had been spared a horrible fate. They could continue their journey without fear of the Sioux. Relations with the Indians were saved. God was watching over the expedition.

As the weather turned chilly, the boats traveled through the Dakotas. Rugged, rocky canyons and rolling plains lined the river. Herds of wild buffalo and deer roamed the countryside. Sunsets of bright orange and yellow capped each day. The scenery was breathtaking.

The expedition stopped for the winter at a village of Mandan Indians in North Dakota. There, they built two barges to replace the keelboat that would return to St. Louis in the spring. They also met Sacagawea, a brown skinned, sixteen-year-old Shoshone Indian squaw, who would take part in the expedition's plans far more than anyone realized.

Winter turned to spring, and the ice melted. Soon the fish were jumping and the buds blooming. The Americans packed up to leave. Lewis and Clark sent the keelboat back to St. Louis, packed with plant and animal specimens. In April, the explorers resumed their journey. Sacagawea and her trapper husband joined them.

The Missouri River turned hostile. With the river too shallow or rocky to paddle or pole, the men pulled out towropes and trudged along the riverbank pulling the barges like pack mules. The work was hard, but their spirits soared as the country unfolded before them. Herds of antelope, moose, and elk grazed on the prairie grasses. Wide rivers snaked along the flat valleys, and huge boulders of rock jabbed the sky.

Day after day, the men poled and pulled. They were out of the barges and canoes more often than they were in them. Before long, the company encountered Great Falls, a 90-foot, roaring wall of water in the Missouri. And then they arrived at the gateway to the mountains. Perpendicular cliffs of black granite towered above them. Majestic, snow-peaked mountains lay before them. The men crossed the deep, scenic gorge and entered the foothills of the Rockies.

The adventurers ascended the great mountain range. On July 25, they traced the source of the Missouri to three small rivers joining together. The men named these rivers the Jefferson, the Madison, and the Gallatin. Excitedly, they pushed up the Jefferson.

The journey grew more torturous than ever. The cold waters of the Jefferson River turned shallow and rapid. The men now hauled their boats by hand. Prickly pear bushes along the banks pierced their wet moccasins and made their feet bleed. Downpours of hailstones bruised and bloodied them. Boils and blisters covered their bodies. Their spirits sank lower and lower. But God had not forgotten them. Sacagawea soon began to recognize the terrain.

"We're nearing Shoshone country!" she exclaimed. "They will help you. They'll have horses that will take you through the mountains."

Captain Lewis scouted ahead for Indians. On August 12, 1805, he and his squad reached the western Continental Divide. They scarcely paused long enough to realize where they were. The Continental Divide stands at the summit of the Rockies, 7,373 feet above sea level. It divides the waters flowing east into the Gulf and the Atlantic from the waters flowing west into the Pacific. But the men were too tired and hungry to care as they clambered down the western slope. They had to find help.

And they did. A group of Shoshone squaws escorted the strangers back to their village. The Shoshone's chief turned out to be Sacagawea's brother! Everyone rejoiced at the delightful surprise. Just as Sacagawea had promised, her people gladly sold horses to the explorers.

The explorers set out again, picking their way through the mountain range, pushing northwest. Frequently, they dismounted to guide their horses along the frightening, gloomy cliffs. As September turned into October, snowstorms beseiged them, and their food almost gave out. Shooting through rocky rapids, the team used the waters of the Columbia River as a roadway. Finally, one dreary day in November 1805, the river widened into a bay.

"Ocean in view! Oh, the joy!" exclaimed Clark in his journal. "There's great joy in camp. We're in view of the great Pacific Ocean. The noise made by the waves breaking on the rocky shores can be heard everywhere!" The expedition spent the winter on the shores of the Pacific and returned to St. Louis in September of 1806.

Lewis and Clark had done it! They had traveled an incredible 4,155 miles overland to the Pacific. Their expedition stood as a monument to the spirit of the American pioneer. It also opened the floodgates for others to pour into the rugged wilderness west of the Mississippi. Soon, mountain men and trappers would roam across the plains. Later, hundreds of canvas-covered wagons would roll westward on the major trails. God had destined America to stretch from sea to shining sea.

CHAPTER
SIX

How blessed are those . . .
Who walk in the law of the LORD. (Psalms 119:1)

CHIEF JUSTICE

Horse-drawn buggies and supply wagons crowded the dusty streets. Fashionably dressed women in colorful bonnets and parasols strolled along the wooden sidewalks, while slaves balanced string-tied bundles on their heads. Men in waistcoats huddled together, smoking cigars and discussing the issues of the day. It was market day in Richmond, Virginia.

One particular Virginian enjoyed his regular outing into town to stock up on supplies. His name was John Marshall. Dressed in ill-fitting clothes, the tall, lanky man looked more like a scarecrow than a gentleman. But he had many friends, and on this market day, was exchanging greetings with a number of them. Suddenly, a stranger, who was visiting the city, approached the lively group.

"Sir," he inquired, addressing Marshall, "would you be so kind as to carry this turkey I've just purchased?" The stranger retrieved a small coin from the front pocket of his vest. Marshall's companions watched silently. The newcomer added, "I'll pay you for your trouble."

The tall Virginian tilted his head as he thought. Without a word, Marshall winked at his friends and nodded yes to the visitor. With the bird tucked under his arm, the employee followed his new boss down the street. Marshall's friends clapped their hands over their mouths to keep from giving him away. As soon as the two men got out of sight, the group roared with laughter. The visitor had just employed the Chief Justice of the United States Supreme Court to carry a turkey!

The United States Supreme Court is the highest court in the land. The Court occupies the third branch of the United States government,while the President and Congress occupy the other two branches. Yet, at the turn of the nineteenth century, political debate raged over the power of the Court. The authority of the Constitution as the supreme law of the land had not yet been established. Men like John Marshall envisioned a strong republic, knitted together by its Constitution and built on the law. They were called Federalists. Others, like Marshall's cousin Thomas Jefferson, believed that a government that governs least governs best. Jefferson was a member of the Democratic-Republican party. Like other members of the party, he favored decreasing the power of government.

How much power did the Constitution delegate to Congress? This was an important issue. During the administrations of George Washington and John Adams, Federalists in Congress introduced legislation to strengthen the federal government. They established an army, created a national bank, and set up the federal court system. By 1800, Americans were demanding more individual and state rights. Popular sentiment spun around from the Federalists to the Democratic Republicans. In the election that year, the Federalists lost both the presidency and their majority in Congress. Thomas Jefferson and the Democratic Republicans took control.

However, just before leaving office, Federalist President John Adams appointed a Chief Justice who also advocated a strong federal government. This was John Marshall. It was this Chief Justice who laid the solid legal foundation for our American system of justice. Through him, God created a country ruled by law.

During the winter of 1803, the Court met in a cramped, basement room in the north wing of the Capitol building in Washington. Chief Justice Marshall and his six associates sat behind the long, polished hardwood bench. They were listening to oral arguments in the case of *Marbury versus Madison.*

This case arose in 1801 after outgoing President Adams appointed Federalist supporters to positions as federal judges. The new President, Thomas Jefferson, ordered Secretary of State James Madison to cancel these commissions. William Marbury, one appointee, sued Madison, and the case of *Marbury versus Madison* made its way onto the docket of the Supreme Court.

In 1803, Marshall issued the Court's decision. Although Marbury was entitled to the appointment, the Court could not reinstate him because his case rested on a law that violated the Constitution. In his decision, Marshall set two precedents that changed the American system of law. He declared that the Constitution was the supreme law of the land. And he established the right of the Court to review all laws passed by Congress.

The fight was on. Neither Congress nor the President was going to let the Court get away with this! Immediately, the House of Representatives took action. It initiated impeachment proceedings against an associate justice on the Court, Samuel Chase. Chase had issued some unwise decisions earlier, and Congress now decided to hold him accountable. The stench of dirty politics hung over the proceedings. Everyone knew what Congress was up to. It wanted to weaken the Supreme Court by asserting its right to remove judges for political reasons.

The congressional debates about Justice Chase dragged on for months. On March 1, 1805, Capitol Hill swarmed with journalists and observers. That day, the Senate would vote. People pushed through the rotunda, the circular area under the capitol dome, and scurried toward the Senate chamber. They crowded into the gallery. As the Senate secretary started to speak, everyone grew quiet.

"How say you?" he asked loudly, addressing the entire chamber. "Is Samuel Chase guilty of high crimes and misdemeanors, as charged in the article just read?" The secretary turned toward the Senator from Massachusetts, whose name topped to roll. "John Quincy Adams!" he called out.

"Not guilty!" Adams replied.

Whispers rustled through the gallery. The secretary continued. When the voting was completed, he announced, "It

is my duty to declare that Samuel Chase stands acquitted!"
The gallery erupted with commotion. Chase was innocent.
The vote had assured the independence of the Supreme
Court.

Who was this popular fourth Chief Justice of the
Supreme Court? John Marshall was a tall, stately Virginian
who greeted others with a twinkle in his eye and a joke on
his lips. Although humble and gentle by nature, he pos-
sessed one of the keenest legal minds ever known. Lawyers
considered the opportunity to argue before him the high
point of their careers. They would spend weeks in prepara-
tion. A legend in his own time, Marshall stood for truth
and justice. His sharp, quick mind could spot error in a
moment. He adored debating principles and legal theories,
but he loved truth even more. And this is what made him
such a great man.

Yet, outside the courtroom, Marshall truly enjoyed being
with people. He liked nothing better than entertaining
friends at home or stopping by a tavern to dine with his
family and other guests. His easy manner and gracious wit
made everyone feel at ease with him, whether they knew
him or not. And his stories brought tears of laughter to his
listeners' eyes. They would beg for more.

Marshall's wit was amazing. One time, he visited a club
in Philadelphia. The club had a rule that its guests had to
make up a rhyme on whatever word was suddenly called
out. As Marshall entered the club to attend a meeting, he
noticed several Kentucky colonels drinking at the bar.

When he walked into his meeting room, someone asked him to provide a rhyme for the word "paradox." Glancing across the hall, he immediately replied:

> In the bluegrass region,
> a paradox is born:
> the corn was full of kernels,
> and the colonels, full of corn.

Although the Chief Justice never publicly spoke about his relationship with the Lord, one incident illustrates the depth of his devotion. Following an accident in his gig, the justice arrived at an inn in Virginia. He decided to spend the night while his buggy was being repaired. That evening, he visited a local tavern. Sitting by himself, the elderly statesman listened to a conversation among some young men.

"Robert, you can't believe Christ was actually the Son of God now, can you?" one fellow asked as he passed around a pitcher. "That's quite absurd, you know."

"I'm not so sure," his companion responded.

"It's one thing to say a man was a great teacher," another argued. "But it's something else to claim he was God."

Finally, one of the gentlemen turned to address the Chief Justice. "Well, my old gentleman," he inquired, "what do you think about these things?"

Marshall leaned forward and placed his arms on the round table in front of him. "Sir," he replied, "I'm glad you asked."

For the next hour, Marshall delivered one of the most eloquent speeches the men had ever heard. Everyone listened as the judge answered the arguments against the teachings of Christ. His listeners marveled at the power of his words. Some thought he was a preacher. No one considered he might be the Chief Justice of the United States Supreme Court. How surprised they were when they found out!

It was winter of 1819, and the cold penetrated the basement of the Capitol building. As the court clerk stoked the fire in the corner Franklin stove, the seven black-robed justices nestled their cold feet in pillows and foot warmers hidden beneath their bench. Visitors wrapped their cloaks and outer coats around them. They could almost see the lawyer's breath as he addressed the high court, presenting arguments in the case of *McCullough versus Maryland.*

This case arose when the Baltimore branch of the Second Bank of the United States refused to pay a tax levied by the state of Maryland. The state had imposed an annual tax of $15,000, but the bank's cashier, James McCullough, refused to pay it. The case went before the Supreme Court. Daniel Webster, a young lawyer from New Hampshire, opened on behalf of the bank.

"The state of Maryland has placed a tax on a national bank," Webster began. "What this means is that a state has imposed a tax on the federal government itself."

The handsome lawyer straightened his vest and pulled his black knee-length coat together at the waist. The gold buttons on his coat glimmered in the candlelight. He continued.

"If the state of Maryland can tax a branch of the national bank, then it can easily put the national bank out of business." Webster's strong voice carried across the room as his deep-set eyes looked straight at the seven justices. "To give the states this kind of power could destroy our federal system. The power to tax is the power to destroy!"

Marshall and the Court agreed with Webster. On March 6, 1819, the Chief Justice delivered the decision in favor of the bank.

"The Constitution has given Congress the right to tax," Marshall declared. "The Constitution and its laws control the laws of the states. State law does not control the Constitution.

"In this case, the law of a state and the law of the federal government conflict. The Constitution directs that federal law must prevail."

Marshall had done it. He had decreed that the government of the United States was a form of national covenant. No one section of America could dictate to the whole. Six states immediately objected to the decision. But, at that precise moment in March 1819, another matter caught everyone's attention. The Missouri Territory's application for statehood ignited a fire of controversy over the question of slavery. Rumors of civil war haunted the nation. The Chief Justice realized that now, more than ever, America needed to be grounded in the law of its Constitution.

When *Cohens versus Virginia* arose, Marshall hammered in the final nail.

Two men named Cohen had been caught selling lottery tickets in the city of Norfolk, Virginia. Virginia law prohibited the selling of such tickets. However, Congress had empowered the city of Washington to run a lottery for raising funds. When the Virginia state court convicted the two men, they appealed their case to the Supreme Court.

Could the verdict of a state court in a criminal case be appealed to a higher national court? This was the question. And the Supreme Court answered yes.

"To take away this right of appeal would deprive the federal judiciary of its authority. The national government would lay prostrate at the feet of every state in the Union," Marshall declared. Then he went on, "The people made the Constitution, and the people can unmake it. It is the creature of their own will, and lives only by their will. This supreme power resides only in the whole body of the people, not in any subdivision of them." The Supreme Court was hereby declaring that the state courts could not have the final say in a case, that the federal courts could overrule them. To drive home his point, Marshall added. "The constitution and laws of a state that violate the Constitution and laws of the United States are absolutely void."

For nearly 20 years, Marshall had been sculpting a republic based on law. His vision never changed. Marshall had declared, beyond any doubt, that the states must obey the Constitution. America was a nation of law.

As Justice Story, who served with him, once said, "John Marshall would have been a great man in any age. He was one of those who stands out like a beacon of light to guide future generations, as well as the present."

And he had guided them well. America was now a covenant people, committed by law to living together as a national family. Her Constitution was supreme. Even the gathering storm of a civil war could not take away this vision. God Almighty was preserving His plan.

One last story illustrated the love Americans held for their fourth Chief Justice. It is said that the Liberty Bell received its crack in 1835, when it tolled in mourning for the death of this great man.

CHAPTER
SEVEN

Do not fear or be dismayed because of this great multitude,
for the battle is not yours but God's. (2 Chronicles 20:15)

"DON'T GIVE UP THE SHIP!"

The blue flag with white stars on it shone in the first rays of the morning sun. An offshore wind straightened the flag as the *USS Chesapeake* set course from Norfolk, Virginia, for the Mediterranean. The ship had a fresh-scrubbed look as mates shouted orders and barefoot sailors scrambled up the rigging to unfurl the mainsails. As the vessel gathered speed, its heavy canvas billowed out and the three masts creaked. The bow rose and fell in the rhythm of the sea, and the ship's lines hummed as it ran with the wind.

Commodore James Barron, the commander, stood on the quarterdeck. "Clear the decks quickly," he ordered. The first lieutenant shouted the order to the boatswain's mate, who instructed the crew to clear the decks.

The commander had no reason to feel uneasy, but he did. The date in the ship's log was June 22, 1807. With the exception of some pirates along the Barbary Coast in North Africa, America had not fired a shot at enemies in more than twenty years. Still, the *Chesapeake* was a man-of-war and must be ready for action at all times.

"Sail ho!" the lookout suddenly shouted.

"Where away?" the first lieutenant cried back.

"Two points off the larboard bow and closing," the lookout yelled.

Commodore Barron nodded to his first lieutenant, who then climbed partway up the rigging and extended his spyglass. In a few moments, he called down, "A frigate, sir, about forty-four guns. Appears to be British."

"Thank you," the commodore replied as a wrinkle formed on his brow.

During the early 1800s, Britain was desperate for men to serve in her navy. Napoleon had conquered all Europe and was planning to invade England. The only way he could be countered was by blockading the entire continent of Europe. Britain started kidnapping sailors and pressing them into service. But conditions in the Royal Navy were so poor that many sailors deserted. So Britain began stopping American merchant ships on the high seas and taking away any sailors who spoke with British accents. Despite America's outrage, the British government did little to prohibit these raids.

Barron gripped the rail tightly. A salty ocean spray gently washed his face as he watched the tiny dot on the horizon swell. Three months earlier, two groups of British seamen had stolen longboats and deserted their frigate in Norfolk harbor. Four of them had volunteered for service on the *Chesapeake*. Three were American citizens, but the fourth, Jenkin Ratford, was a British tailor who had been impressed in London. Up to this point, the British had never stopped an American naval vessel. Were they about to do it now?

As the dot grew, the American commander sensed trouble. He was right. It turned out that British Vice Admiral Sir George Berkeley had sent his own flagship, *HMS Leopard*, to find the *Chesapeake* and search her for British deserters.

The *Leopard* reached the American ship and pulled alongside. A lieutenant, sent over in a longboat, presented the British demands.

"Tell your captain I'll not release any of my men," Barron replied.

The British lieutenant climbed back into the longboat. As soon as he was off the deck, Barron signaled, "All hands, ready for action!"

Suddenly, the *Leopard's* captain shouted above the sea winds, "Commodore Barron!" The American commander turned around. "Release the British deserters to me, or I'll come aboard, muster the crew, and get them myself!"

"Only the captain or first lieutenant can muster an American crew aboard an American warship, sir," Barron responded just as loudly.

"Fire!" the British officer ordered. The *Leopard* fired its cannon at pointblank range into the side of the American frigate. The *Chesapeake* staggered under the impact. The *Leopard* then shot a second broadside, and a third. The *Chesapeake* had not been able to return a single shot. With three men dead and eighteen wounded, the American commander struck his colors and surrendered. The British impressed all four men and sailed back to Nova Scotia.

Outrage swept the eastern seaboard. U.S. newspapers condemned the action. "War hawks" in Congress—fiery young congressmen from the south and west—demanded war. President Jefferson did not want war, yet he could not permit the British to kidnap American seamen. In December 1807, Jefferson convinced Congress to pass the Embargo Act and prohibit American exports. Jefferson hoped to force England to cooperate by stopping U.S. merchant ships from sailing to foreign ports. But his plan failed miserably. New England shipyards closed down. Bales of cotton piled high on southern docks. Produce from western farms rotted on the docks in New Orleans. Shipowners and merchants selling goods to Britain and France lost their patience. Threats of secession crossed many lips, and Congress repealed the hated Embargo Act.

But the impressment of American sailors by the British continued. And British support of Indian uprisings in the Northwest Territory only added fuel to the smoldering fire. In 1812, relations between Britain and the United States collapsed. On June 18, President James Madison formally declared war.

The initial American strategy focused on Canada. The United States hoped to prevent a British military thrust from the north. British forces still occupied a number of forts in Canada, near the border. Instead of launching one major offensive, the United States planned a three-prong attack. The first two attempts failed miserably with U.S. forces surrendering at Detroit and Niagara. The third assault concentrated on Lake Erie, the "inland sea" that separated the United States from Canada.

Positioned on either end of this huge lake were the British garrisons at Detroit and Niagara. The enemy could easily invade the United States with its armed brigantines. The Americans had to seize control. But their tiny navy of sixteen warships could hardly withstand a full British onslaught. The ranking officer on Lake Erie, Lieutenant Oliver Hazard Perry, decided to do something about it. He constructed a squadron at Erie, two large brigs of 480 tons each and two support ships. But he needed sailors to man the new ships. The twenty-seven-year-old officer went to Brigadier General William Henry Harrison, commander of the Army of the Northwest.

Lieutenant Oliver Hazard Perry approached the big, oak door with his heart pounding. He wore his dress blues. A shiny new sword hung at his left side from the belt. He had to look good today. It was an important day. He was about to meet the Brigadier General. But what if the general wouldn't listen? What if he refused to give Perry more men? The lieutenant would not think about this now. He had a job to do. The young man swallowed hard and knocked on the door.

"Come in," answered a low voice from inside.

Perry twisted the brass doorknob and pushed open the heavy door. He walked inside.

The Brigadier General stood in front of a large map hanging on the wall. He was a thin man with gray hair, a long, pointed nose, and deep-set eyes. As Perry entered, the general turned to greet his visitor.

"Yes?" he said.

The lieutenant saluted. "Sir, I'm Lieutenant Oliver Perry. I've come to discuss a matter of grave concern."

"At ease, Lieutenant," General Harrison answered. "I've been waiting for your arrival. Please sit down. I'm very interested in what you're doing on Lake Erie."

"Thank you, sir," Perry responded, dropping into a nearby chair.

"Tell me, Lieutenant, how's the building coming?"

"Well, sir, we've almost finished the two larger ships, the *Lawrence* and the *Niagara*. And we're working on the two support ships. Work is going smoothly. But I need your help. I don't have enough men to outfit these ships. I need some seamen."

"Ah," Harrison replied, shaking his head sadly. "That's a big order. The United States navy is so small. We just don't have enough trained sailors. I'm afraid I don't have them to give to you."

"General, I've been thinking about that," Perry replied as he sat up in the chair, his sword now touching the floor. "If you could send me some riflemen, I could train them as seamen and marines."

"That might be a possibility," the grizzled, old brigadier replied thoughtfully. "What exactly do you propose to do with them?"

"With these vessels I'm building, the American fleet will be roughly equal in tonnage to the British. This will increase our chances of taking Lake Erie. As I see it, it's very important that we take the lake right away. Napoleon is suffering some major defeats, and his allies are no longer standing with him. This means that Britain is gaining support. If this happens, Britain may soon send General

Wellington to North America. Right now, the British force in Canada is small. But this won't continue. And, if the British do send the 'Iron Duke', British morale will soar. General, I don't think we can take the chance. We must secure Erie right away."

Harrison appreciated the delicate, shifting balance of power in Europe and the need for immediate action. Without hesitation, he drafted dozens of crewmen from his ranks for Perry's ships. Perry also received 100 of his finest Kentucky marksmen. A triumphant lieutenant returned to the lake.

By the beginning of August, they had finished the new brigs. Gunnery practice became the first order of each day. Perry drilled his new crews until he could count on them to fire rapidly and accurately, even at close range. At first, the landlubbers had trouble adapting to the disciplines of naval warfare. But Perry worked patiently with them until they understood the precise, demanding responsibilities of combat at sea.

By mid-August, they were ready. Perry anchored the squadron just outside the mouth of the Detroit river. British Captain Robert Barclay positioned his fleet in the middle of the river, hoping for a standoff. Maybe an early December freeze would immobilize both fleets and give Wellington time to sail from Europe with reinforcements.

Several times in late August, Perry stationed his fleet at the mouth of the river, hoping to bait the enemy into a fight. When it did not work, the lieutenant decided to go in after them. He summoned his captains to a council of war.

The men stood around the chart table as Perry pointed out the positions on the map.

"Each of you has been assigned a specific ship in the British squadron," Perry began. "I want you to seek out that ship and destroy her.

"Captain Elliott, the *Niagara* will line up against the British *Queen Charlotte*."

"Aye, aye, sir. I'll reduce her to floating wreckage in ten minutes," Elliott boasted.

"I'll be aboard the *Lawrence*. We'll fight the new British flagship, the *Detroit*." Perry paused. "It's time for battle!"

The morning of September 10 dawned bright and clear. As the ships tacked out of the bay, 6 British frigates greeted them on the horizon, in line of battle. The Americans had 9 ships and 54 guns. The British had 6 ships and 63 guns. Perry knew that enemy firepower was far more important than their extra schooners. Perry glanced up at the pennants on the masts.

"We've got a southwest wind," he said to his sailing master. "The British will have the advantage with the wind on their side."

The sailing master just smiled. "No matter which way the wind's blowin', sir, they shall fight today!"

"Clear for action!" the first lieutenant yelled.

The crew cleared away the extra gear. They hung hammocks inside the bulkheads to cut down some of the large flying shrapnel. Then they tossed sand on the decks. Fresh blood was slippery, and there would be a lot of it today. At last, everything was ready.

Three hours remained until the wind would finally bring the two fleets broadside. At 10:30 A.M., Perry ordered a meal served to the men at their battle stations. As the sailors finished, they heard a bugle sound across the water. The British band had struck up the national anthem, "Rule Britannia." The Americans scanned the enemy's flags and freshly painted hulls. It was an imposing sight.

But Captain Perry held a surprise of his own. "Hoist the flag!" he ordered. Immediately, two mates raised a big flag with the words DON'T GIVE UP THE SHIP. The sailors cheered as they recognized the words said by Captain Lawrence before he died on the *Chesapeake* five years before.

At 11:50 , the long guns on the *Detroit* opened fire on the *Lawrence*. They hit the target. From the quarterdeck, Perry steadied his crew, reminding them that they would have their chance, soon enough. However, something was wrong. The battle lines were not coming together as Perry had planned. The *Lawrence* had to sail down the entire British line before coming abreast of the *Detroit*. Enemy guns could concentrate on her alone.

Time seemed to come to a standstill as the entire British fleet poured its fire into the *Lawrence*. Chaos seized the ship's main deck. Men screamed as shrapnel pelted the deck and hit them. The canvas and rigging fell. Guns were knocked off their carriages. Perry passed the word to take the wounded below to the surgeon. The decks ran red with blood.

Yet the *Lawrence* inflicted some heavy damage of her own. Perry had released his gun captains to choose their targets, and the gunners chose well. One by one, they aimed, put their torches to the torchholes, clapped their hands over their ears, and fired. Then they reloaded and waited for an enemy gun or mast or rudder to come into sight.

"Mr. Yarnell," Perry cried in despair. "Where's the *Niagara?*"

"To leeward, sir. She seems to be holding out of range."

"Well, signal her up here, mister!"

The executive officer ordered the bugler to signal their sister ship, but the *Niagara* did not respond. Furious, Perry directed the fire of their last three guns. The endless hours of practice now paid off. As the *Lawrence* drifted astern, the incoming rounds from the *Detroit* and *Queen Charlotte* diminished.

The American flagship drifted rudderless in the water. All was quiet. British Commander Barclay peered through his spyglass from the quarterdeck of the *Detroit*. "Surely Perry will strike his colors now and lower the flag," the officer commented to his first mate.

But Perry had not yet given up. With the help of two unwounded men, Perry loaded the one gun that was left. He aimed it at the *Detroit*'s quarterdeck and fired. The shot hit a bull's eye, and Barclay died.

An hour had passed. Perry realized that the *Niagara* had switched positions, setting the *Lawrence* between herself and the British frigates! In a cold rage, he exploded, "I'll go there, take command of her, and sail her into battle myself! Mr. Yarnell, don't strike colors until I'm well clear."

With that, the commander hauled down the flag. Tucking it under his arm, he signaled to lower the longboat for use. Four seamen rowed Perry furiously across the water as shot and musket balls rained down around them.

Perry climbed aboard the *Niagara*. "Raise the flag! I've been sacrificed!" he shouted at Captain Elliott, who stared at him as if he were seeing a ghost.

"Sir, I'll take the boat and go fetch the two schooners lagging behind," Elliott sheepishly suggested.

Perry gladly let him go and immediately took command of the *Niagara*. As he hoisted her sail, the ship leapt forward in the water. The sailors cheered.

"Double load. Stand by all guns. Fire as your guns bear!" he commanded from the quarterdeck.

In eight minutes, three British frigates lay dead in the water. The battle was over. With trembling hand, Perry penned a brief dispatch to Brigadier General Harrison.

> We have met the enemy, and they are ours: two
> ships, two brigs, one schooner, and one sloop.
> Yours, with greatest respect and esteem,
> O. H. Perry

He sent a second note to the Secretary of the Navy.

> It has pleased the Almighty to give the United
> States a victory over their enemies on this lake. The
> British squadron have this moment surrendered to
> the force of my command.

As Perry looked astern at the floating hulk of the *Lawrence*, he realized he had come through the battle without being hurt. The commander bowed his head and whispered, "The prayers of my wife are answered."

Perry's victory at Erie turned the tide of the northwest campaign in favor of the Americans. America celebrated its victory. Yet no one publicly gave thanks to the One who had delivered them. Once again, the republic seemed to be forgetting God. And this was not good, for the war with the British was far from over.

He broke the flaming arrows,
The shield, and the sword, and the weapons of war. (Psalms 76:3)

THE DAWN'S EARLY LIGHT

It was early morning in Baltimore, Maryland. The sunlight bathed the harbor in a soft golden haze. It touched the roofs of the clapboard houses nestled around the bay. Everything was quiet except for the harbor. Six, sleek gunships glided through the morning mist. Silently, they passed by the fort guarding the harbor. A sentinel waved to them, but the sailors were too busy to wave back. They had an important job to do. They were tacking out to sea in search of British ships.

After the victory on Lake Erie, morale in America soared, but not for long. In the winter of 1813-14, Napoleon was toppled from power in Europe. Britain could now concentrate its power elsewhere, and this meant America. Ever since the War for Independence, the British attitude toward the new nation had been proud and defiant. Americans realized that Britain would like nothing better than to teach the new nation a lesson or two.

But the Americans had something up their sleeve, and

this was the privateers. Privateers were private warships hired to attack and capture enemy ships. Most of them weighed anchor at Baltimore and set a course for the Irish Sea. They hunted solo and in small groups, sinking or capturing British vessels. In 1814, the *Perry* captured 22 British frigates on a two-month cruise, while the *Governor Tompkin* seized 14 ships in a single sweep through the British Channel. The British were not happy.

The British retaliated by raiding and robbing every undefended coastal town along the East Coast. In 1814, a squadron of British ships raided the shore towns of Maryland. On August 24, Major General Robert Ross and Rear Admiral Sir George Cockburn led British troops toward Washington from the mouth of the Patuxent River. The Americans were not ready to fight, and by dusk, the British had captured the city. Cockburn torched the Capitol and looted the White House. The night sky over Washington turned an angry red-orange as flames leaped into the sky.

Where was God when this was happening? The British burned much of the capital city, but God did not allow them to destroy it. A sudden thunderstorm put out the flames. The next day, a tornado struck the city, forcing General Ross to retreat to the Patuxent with his troops.

While the British eyed Baltimore, another battle was brewing in the north on Lake Champlain. Lake Champlain is a long, narrow lake between New York and Vermont, stretching into Quebec. A British force of 18,000 troops paused, ready to plunge down the lake and the Hudson River into New York. They hoped to split off New England from the rest of the Union. Thirty-three hundred rag-tag Americans faced this great engine of war.

Yet, one detail kept the British at bay. Anchored in Plattsburg Bay was a small American fleet of four brigs and eight gunboats. Could this fleet help the Yankee cause? Sir George Prevost, the British commander, thought it could. He ordered his naval captain to destroy the fleet. The British captain and his officers sat together as the light of the noonday sun shone through a small porthole behind them. Wild ducks flew overhead, quacking loudly.

"Sir," one officer suggested, "if we coax them out in the open, we'll have the advantage. If we enter the bay—"

"He's right, captain," another interrupted. "The Americans will have an advantage if we lead our flotilla into the bay."

The captain drummed his fingers on the table. "Gentlemen, I share your concerns," he replied, "but Prevost has attacked my character. He called me a coward! I won't stand for that. We're going to attack."

The British captain should have listened to his officers. As the British fleet entered the bay, the wind died down, and the flotilla had to glide past the battle line. The American ships, anchored and holding, could pivot and fire deadly broadsides. In 15 minutes, their mortars had disabled two British craft and killed the captain. A disheartened Prevost observed the action through fieldglasses. He withdrew his army without firing a shot. Eight hundred furious British soldiers deserted to the American side.

Lieutenant John MacDonough, commander of the American gunnery, sent a report to President Madison.

"The Almighty has been pleased to grant us a victory." The United States had sealed off the last invasion route from the north.

In the meantime, British General Ross and Admiral Cockburn were advancing on Baltimore. The Sunday before the attack, a Methodist missionary named Joshua Thomas addressed the British troops. The sun's rays warmed the cool, damp Maryland morning that day as 12,000 British soldiers sat on the grass, listening to his sermon.

"Christ Jesus came into the world to save sinners," the preacher proclaimed. "He saved me from sin, and He wants to save you." Thomas stopped to clear his throat. "The Almighty has told me that you're not going to be able to take Baltimore. Many of you are going to die by the sword. I fear that, for many of you, this is your last call to salvation. Let Christ come into your hearts now. Turn your lives over to Him!"

The British approached Baltimore by land as well as from the Chesapeake Bay. This time, the Yankees stood ready. On land, American General John Stricker lined up three regiments of militia. As soon as they sighted the Redcoats, the Americans opened fire and melted into the woods.

"I'm going back to hurry the infantry," British General Ross announced, wheeling his horse around. Suddenly, a rifle bullet pierced his arm and buried itself into his chest. Ross toppled from his horse into the dust and died.

Arthur Brooke, the British second in command, took over. More than 4,000 veteran Redcoats heaved forward, against 1,700 greenhorn Americans. With fixed bayonets, the Redcoats resembled scarlet ghosts advancing through the smoke. Fear shuddered through the ranks of the waiting Marylanders.

"Hold your fire, men!" a Yankee officer called out to the ranks. "Let 'em get closer! Remember, aim just below the buckle on their chests, and shoot the officers first. Hold steady . . . now, fire!"

A volley roared out. The red line stopped and returned a volley. As the first rank reloaded, the second stepped up, paused, and fired a second volley. The Americans did not win the field that day, but their stiff resistance forced the British to wait for naval support. The battle for Baltimore moved to the sea.

Commanding the entrance to Baltimore's harbor was Fort McHenry, a fortress of vast earthworks shaped like a star and reinforced with logs. Sunken ships created a picket fence of masts in the harbor, causing the British men-of-war to anchor at a distance. The flagship of Vice Admiral Sir Alexander Cochrane, the *HMS Tonnant*, mounted an incredible 90 guns. America's largest ship, the *Constitution*, carried only 44. The British had the fire power, and they hovered, like circling hawks, ready to use it.

On Tuesday, September 13, 1814, the first light of dawn gently burned away the morning mist. Suddenly, the earth-shaking sound of the *Tonnant*'s heavy guns shattered the calm. Deadly mortars poured down on the fort! The British were bombarding the Americans with everything they had.

The incoming shells struck terror in the hearts of the Yankee soldiers. The whistle of their approach and their earth-shaking explosions seemed to turn the world upside down. The soldiers screamed and clawed at the ground. To make things worse, every three or four minutes, a huge mortar round dropped from the sky. But strangely enough, none of them exploded! Instead, they plunged into the mudbanks, which had been softened by rain. The mud soaked the mortar shells up like a sponge. Wisps of gray smoke curled up from their fuse holes. Some simply sputtered out. One even landed directly on top of the fort's powder magazine, denting the roof. Yet, it did not explode. Clearly, God was helping them!

Back on land, British Colonel Brooke opened a sealed envelope in his tent just outside Baltimore. He pulled out the message and read. "Hmmm . . . " he muttered. "Admiral Cochrane wants to land a small force of men by sea to divert the Yanks' attention from our land assault." Brooke nodded his head in agreement. "Lieutenant," he called out, "get the men ready. We attack tonight!"

Once again, things did not go well for the British. That night, a heavy rain blocked the landing party's vision, sending some of them the wrong way. The rain also soaked the guns of Brooke's infantry and prevented the soldiers from using their rifles. To make matters worse, Yankee lookouts at Fort McHenry spied the main British force before it could reach shore. They opened fire, and the British turned back. The surprise assault had failed.

Admiral Cochrane became more determined than ever to destroy the fort. Throughout the night, British bombs burst in the air, and mortars thudded into the muddy embankments of Fort McHenry.

During the attack, a young lawyer from Washington named Francis Scott Key, stood on one of the British warships. Key had boarded the vessel to negotiate an exchange of prisoners. The young man stared at the blazing rockets, arching their fiery missiles into the fort. The night chill sent shivers up his spine. He pulled his cloak more tightly around his shoulders as the thundering booms rang in his ears. At times, the bombs glared so brightly that it looked like daylight. As a rainstorm blew up, Key anxiously strained his eyes for a glimpse of the fort. Was the giant flag still flying?

Key pulled a letter from his pocket and began to scribble some words on the back.

Oh! say, can you see, by the dawn's early light,
What so proudly we hailed at the twilight's last gleaming?
Whose broad stripes and bright stars, thro' the perilous fight.
O'er the ramparts we watched were so gallantly streaming?

As the breeze moistened the paper's edges, the man continued writing. The words flowed easily.

And the rockets' red glare, the bombs bursting in air,
Gave proof thro' the night that our flag was still there.
Oh! say, does that star-spangled banner yet wave
O'er the land of the free and the home of the brave?

When light dawned, the lawyer spotted the huge Stars and Stripes still flying over the fort. Back at the Baltimore Hotel later that day, he put in final form the words that have rooted themselves in the hearts of Americans everywhere as our National Anthem. Today, the "Star Spangled

Banner" stands as a written monument to the courage of a nation and the importance of its flag.

On December 24, 1814, diplomats from the United States and Great Britain gathered in Ghent, Belgium. The events at Lake Champlain and Baltimore persuaded the British to sign a peace treaty. The American ambassadors sent a sloop of war to New York with the news. But it did not reach America in time. Before it could get there, British sails unfurled and ships headed toward New Orleans. Seven thousand British troops under Sir Edward Pakenham had set out to capture the largest trading port in the New World. Yet, one man blocked their path. He was General Andrew Jackson.

Old Hickory stood on the deck of the two-masted schooner as it silently glided along the river near New Orleans. The tall, long-haired general brushed his thick gray locks back under his leather cap and wiped some mud off his unpolished leather boots. It was the night of December 23, 1814. Jackson and his men were combing the riverbank, looking for Pakenham's camp eight miles out of New Orleans.

Unexpectedly, a low-lying fog rolled in. *Splendid!* Jackson thought as he pulled his cap closer to his brow. *This fog will cover our advance. By thunder, we'll give 'em quite a Christmas present now!*

The British were eating supper when the unexpected vessel emerged from the fog. Suddenly, a seven-gun broadside belched fire and filled the air with a hurricane of iron. The Americans were attacking! Tents and stacks of enemy weapons blew into a thousand pieces. Cries of fear marred the Louisiana night. The Redcoats retreated at once. General Jackson had stopped their advance—for now.

The man called Old Hickory was not the kind of general to sit around and see what the enemy would try next. Jackson ordered his men to move south, to a canal five miles below New Orleans on the river. There, they dug trenches and built redoubts, large mounds of mud, to barricade themselves against the enemy. In the meantime, Jackson's ranks swelled with new volunteers from Tennessee and Kentucky, who had come to fight alongside Old Hickory. Soon, 4,000 American troops lay waiting on the east bank, with 1,000 more guarding them across the river.

General Pakenham held a council of war with his top generals. The British officers met in the general's tent. A wooden cot with two wool blankets and a pillow occupied one corner. An arsenal of weapons leaned against his footlocker in the other. The soldiers gathered around a table in the middle.

"Gentlemen, I think we're in agreement," Pakenham said as he summed up their meeting. "We'll lay bundles of sugarcane in the canal in front of the redoubt so we can cross. Then, we'll scale the rampart with ladders. Lieutenant Colonel Mullens and his Forty-fourth Regiment will carry the cane bundles and the scaling ladders."

At midnight on January 8, American sentries spied the first detachment of enemy troops rowing quietly across the river. They roused General Jackson at 1:00 A.M. "Gentlemen," Old Hickory responded, "we've slept enough."

Two hours later, Lieutenant Colonel Mullens was leading his British regiment through the darkness to the forward battery where he expected to find the scaling ladders and cane bundles. But they were not there! Mullens' heart sank when he realized his error. His orders had been to pick the equipment up at the forward redoubt—now some 400 yards behind them—and he had not done it. He sent 300 men back to fetch it, knowing full well they could not possibly return before daybreak.

"Sir, you must break off the attack," Captain Harry Smith pleaded with General Pakenham. "Our thrust across the canal has been lost."

Pakenham shook his head and sighed. "I'll not put this off," he directed. "We'll make a frontal assault in close column formation. Fire the signal rocket."

The Yankees remained ready behind their temporary barriers. "Here they come!" someone yelled.

BOOM! The Americans opened fire. Their cannon punched holes in the first ranks but did not stop the advance. The British kept coming.

Old Hickory turned to General John Adair, "Hold your fire," he ordered. "The smoke from the British artillery will stop the men from finding their marks." An eerie silence followed. Jackson broke the silence. "Gentlemen, they're near enough now. Fire when ready!"

Adair yelled to a Kentucky sharpshooter named Morgan Ballard. "Morg, see that officer on the gray horse?"

The rifleman nodded.

"Snuff his candle!"

Ballard bent to his sight, aimed, and squeezed off a round. The bullet struck the officer just above the ear.

British Major John Anthony Whitaker was dead before he hit the ground.

The British were stunned. That shot had come from more than three hundred yards away! How could this be? Instantly, the first American line burst into fire. Rotating forward, the second column of 150 men aimed and fired. Then the third rank stepped in. Scores of British soldiers plummeted to the ground. It was a massacre.

From his lookout point, Pakenham ordered the Forty-fourth to get their scaling ladders to the ramparts. When no one could find Lieutenant Colonel Mullens, Pakenham led the charge. But a cannonball struck and killed his horse. Pakenham fell to the ground. Struggling to his feet, he grabbed another horse just before two bullets ripped into him. The general died at once.

The only British field officer left alive, General Gibbs, assumed the command. In a rage, the screaming general charged across the field toward the enemy. The waiting Yanks took aim and fired and the general keeled over into the mud. The British troops bolted and ran.

The British had suffered 1,971 casualties while American losses numbered 7 killed and 6 wounded. The War of 1812 was over.

Newspaper headlines trumpeted the news, and the nation went wild with joy. Jackson became a national hero. Banquets, bonfires, and speeches lasted for days. Finally, Europe would have to recognize America's right to independence. The young republic had proven itself to the world.

God had clearly given America the victory. But only one

public figure emphasized His role. "God's hand shielded my men from the shower of balls and bombs," General Jackson wrote. "Heaven intervened wonderfully in our behalf. I am filled with gratitude, when I look back to what we have escaped."

The war was over. It was time for America to rejoice—at least for a while.

CHAPTER

NINE

"Hear this, O foolish and senseless people,
Who have eyes, but see not . . .
Do you not fear Me?" declares the LORD. *(Jeremiah 5:21–22)*

THE ERA OF GOOD FEELINGS

The onlookers shaded their eyes from the sun on that first Tuesday in March 1817. From the risers, they could see the long row of wooden dwellings stretching into the grassy marshland. They strained to view the silvery Potomac, shimmering beyond. In the distance, the elegant White House clashed dramatically with the lowly structures nearby and the magnificent Capitol behind. Potholes and grazing cows dotted the scene.

On this particular day, a dignified assembly had gathered to witness the inauguration of the fifth President of the United States. Congressmen, senators, and cabinet members chatted informally. Invited diplomats and senior military officers stood close by. They gazed at the small, elderly President-elect in his waistcoat and breeches. A flicker of amusement crossed their faces at his old-fashioned dress. But the sun's rays warmed everyone's heart as the man raised his right hand and solemnly received the oath. Spring had come as last.

Everyone's spirits lifted even higher when President James Monroe summed up the country's good feelings. "Our citizens are happy," he declared, "and our nation is prosperous. We are one great family with a common interest. The heart of every citizen must expand with joy, when he reflects on how near our government has approached to perfection. If we continue in the path already traced, we cannot fail, under the favor of a gracious Providence, to attain the high destiny which seems to await us."

God had placed a calling on the United States. He had ordained her to become "one nation under God." He had set her apart as a nation of believers, grounded in His Word and rooted in commitment to His Son. The one true God intended America to shine its light across the globe and illuminate His city set upon a hill.

Following the War of 1812, America's future seemed as bright as that sunny inaugural day in the nation's capital. Yet, a trap of deception lurked beneath all the talk about happiness and prosperity. Mushrooming problems in the banking industry and foreign affairs engulfed Monroe's administration. And the growing disagreement over slavery threatened an earthquake that would shake the very foundations of the country. The Era of Good Feelings was not what it seemed.

George Houston, a young pioneer, surveyed the scene. Yellow wildflowers, blue sage, and white lilies swayed in the meadow in front of him. Oaks, maples, and beech trees mingled together in the woods to the east. A tributary flowing toward the Ohio River ran right through the middle of the property. *Yep*, he nodded to himself, *this here's the place!*

Young Houston had heard that farming was good in Ohio, so he had brought his family out from Pennsylvania. It was the chance for a new life, but he had no money. So he traveled into the nearby town of Zanesville, located on one of the main routes west.

"You say you have no collateral?" the banker inquired.

"No sir," Houston answered, twiddling his straw hat with his fingers and looking down at the floor.

"Well, that's not a problem, young man," the loan officer replied. "You're young and strong. And that farm's going to be worth something some day, isn't it? We'll call your farm 'future collateral'."

"Sir, that's very kind of you," Houston replied.

"Now you sign right here, and we've got 10,000 brand new, Sixth Bank of Zanesville dollars for you! What do you think of that? Won't the missus be pleased!"

The young man signed the paper, called a mortgage. In a mortgage, a lender agrees to loan money, and a borrower agrees to pay this money back with interest. Interest is additional money paid for the right to borrow. It is the lender's profit. George Houston agreed to pay this interest to the bank, in addition to repaying the borrowed amount.

The excited farmer accepted the money, bought the land and purchased the equipment he needed. Over the next year, he worked hard. He built a two-room cabin as well as a wooden shed for his horse and pigs. By year's end, he had cleared six acres and planted two crops of corn and wheat.

One Tuesday, Houston drove his horse and wagon into Zanesville for supplies. After tying the brown mare to a hitching post, he stomped up the dusty steps to the Zanesville Feed & Grain. Joe Randolph, the store owner, was busy arranging candy jars on a shelf behind the counter. Two other customers were browsing around the store. Houston walked up to the counter.

"Morning, Mr. Randolph," Houston said, cheerfully. "I'm needin' some more supplies."

"Good mornin' to ya, Mr. Houston," Randolph replied, wiping his hands on his white apron. "What can I get fer ya?"

"I need fifty pounds of grain, five pounds of sugar and ten pounds of flour. I'd also like two sticks of your cinnamon candy for my young'uns."

Randolph retrieved the items as Houston wandered around. "How about adding ten pounds of salt?" the farmer hollered from one of the aisles.

"Mr. Houston, your order's ready," the storekeeper announced.

"What's it come to?" the farmer asked as he approached the counter.

"$18.76."

Houston pulled the Zanesville dollars out of his wallet and laid the amount on the counter.

"I'm sorry, Mr. Houston," Randolph uttered. "This won't cover it."

"What!" Houston blurted back. "These are good dollars, issued by the Sixth Bank of Zanesville! What d'ya mean, they won't cover it!"

"Mr. Houston, I can only give you fifty cents on the dollar for this money. It's lost value. If you use it, you'll have to pay me $37.52."

The angry young farmer slammed the money on the counter and left. After loading his supplies on the wagon, he marched over to the Sixth Bank of Zanesville. The news was not good. The Sixth Bank had sold out to another bank. In fact, there were now 176 banks in the one Ohio town. This new bank had bought Houston's mortgage. The farmer discovered that he now owed twice as much in interest. The fact that his Sixth Bank of Zanesville dollars had dropped in value did not worry the new bank. "You'll just have to work harder, and pay us more," the loan officer advised, "or we'll call your loan." If that happened, Houston knew he would lose everything.

The next year, Houston did work hard, but he could not work hard enough. He was fighting a losing battle. His Sixth Bank of Zanesville money dwindled down to twenty cents on the dollar. Before long, the bank gave him two weeks to get off the property. Houston took his family and slipped out of town, just one step ahead of the sheriff.

What happened to George Houston and his family was happening all over the country, especially out west in towns like Zanesville, Ohio. When Congress failed to renew the charter of the nation's first national bank, state banks multiplied throughout the land. These banks set their own rules for banking. Individual banks printed their own notes and promised to exchange these notes for gold or silver, on demand. Customers could bring their notes to the bank and receive either gold or silver in return at any time. This practice would have been fine had the banks kept enough gold and silver coins. But most did not. And many lent money at such high interest rates, folks could not repay. The banking industry plunged into chaos. Bank notes lost their value, and depositors lost their money.

In 1816, Congress chartered a second national bank, the Second Bank of the United States. Yet, state banks continued their dishonest practices. By 1819, nearly 40 percent of the money in circulation was counterfeit. Racketeers printed money on imaginary banks in other states and then skipped town before anyone could find out.

The United States economy spiraled into a depression. Currency with value almost evaporated altogether. Merchants could not sell their goods. Factories laid off their employees. In Philadelphia alone, three-fourths of the workers were let go in the year 1819. When the head office of the Second Bank called in its loans, an economic panic engulfed the nation. Before it was over, thousands of businesses had been ruined.

These underhanded bank dealings were only part of the troubles facing the nation during the Era of Good Feelings. What should be done about Spanish-owned Florida? Bands of Seminole Indians were now swarming across the Florida border into southern Georgia and raiding the settlers. Georgians pleaded with the government to do something. The government formally protested to Spain, but nothing happened.

Andrew Jackson watched all this from his home in Tennessee. On the day of Monroe's inauguration, Old Hickory sat on the front porch of the Hermitage, getting ready to write a letter about the situation.

"Monroe and I think alike," the crusty commander muttered to himself. "He'll want to do something about this. He realizes that any foreign power holding Florida points a gun at the heart of the South." Jackson unbuttoned his buckskin jacket and scooted his chair toward the desk. "I can clean out them Seminoles. Can't be no more trouble than cleanin' out the Redcoats on my way to New Orleans."

The commander dispatched a letter, but he never received a reply. Urgently, he sent another. "Something must be done! Give me the word, and I'll do it."

Could the President of the United States sanction an invasion into friendly territory? President Monroe was not sure. He knew he did not want a war, but he wrote back to Jackson: "There is no time to rest, until our cause is carried triumphantly through."

The President's words signaled action! Immediately, Jackson summoned his officers and raised an army. He even advanced $4,000 of his own money to pay the expenses of the march. They were on their way to Florida at last.

On March 10, 1818, Jackson's militia tramped across the border. They waded through swamps filled with mosquitoes toward the Indians' camps. The Seminoles fled before them into two Spanish forts. Jackson first marched to San Marcos, in east Florida, where he hanged two Indian chiefs. Next, he stormed San Michel in west Florida, near the panhandle. The siege took eighty days.

Washington skyrocketed into rage. America now faced the horrendous possibility of another war, this time with Spain. President Monroe denied authorizing the invasion, and Jackson was called a liar. The general raced to the capital to clear his name.

On July 15, President Monroe summoned his cabinet to the White House. The members gathered in the meeting room like nervous squirrels who had just heard a loud bark. John Calhoun, the Secretary of War, and William Crawford, the Secretary of the Treasury, whispered in a corner. Daniel Tomkins poured himself a cool drink. The Attorney General and Secretary of the Navy consulted near the window. Secretary of State John Adams sat and waited. Finally, the President called the meeting to order.

After agreeing to return the forts to Spain, the cabinet focused its attention on the hardest question of all. What should they do about Jackson? For five long hours, the men argued. For one reason or another, most of them wanted to punish Jackson in some way.

But Secretary of State Adams defended the general's actions. "I explained to Don Louis de Onis, the Spanish ambassador, that we could not sit by while our women and children were being butchered. General Jackson wasn't waging a war. He was defending American lives."

The cabinet sided with Adams. It realized Spain had no interest in war with the United States. Rebelling colonies in South America required her attention at that time. In addition, the cabinet recognized Jackson's soaring popularity since the Florida campaign. Like it or not, Old Hickory had become the most popular man in the country. Voting against him would mean political suicide. The cabinet decided to leave him alone.

A third problem plagued America during this Era of Good Feelings. This one centered on international relations, too. But God provided an able statesman and negotiator to guide the nation's actions. His name was John Quincy Adams.

As the only son of John Adams, second President of the United States, young Adams had been raised in a strong Puritan background. Like the Puritans, Adams considered public service a high calling from God. Although he never actively sought public life, John Quincy Adams served his country well. He acted as ambassador to Russia and England. He negotiated the Treaty of Ghent in 1812, and eventually, he was elected sixth President of the United States.

As Monroe's Secretary of State, Adams achieved two diplomatic milestones in America's history. In 1819, he reached an agreement with Spain known as the Transcontinental Treaty. Spain agreed to cede Florida to the United States as well as to pay damages to American citizens harmed by the Seminoles. She also agreed to give up her claims to the territory north of the forty-second parallel (the southern border of Oregon and Idaho today). In exchange, the United States yielded its claims to the Texas territory and California. The two nations signed the Transcontinental Treaty, extending the United States border from the Sabine River to the Pacific Ocean. As a result of Adams' work, the country truly stretched from one sea to the other.

The Secretary of State considered this treaty the highlight of his career. Four years later, he helped draft another important document. This was the Monroe Doctrine, and it remains a cornerstone of foreign policy to this day.

Once again, the circumstances involved Spain. During the early nineteenth century, Spain's empire in the New World included Central America, South America, and the Caribbean. By 1822, however, most of her South American colonies had revolted and declared their independence. Like their neighbor to the north, these colonies yearned for freedom. Armed with the support of her European allies, Spain threatened to use force to regain her rule.

This alarmed the United States and England. The United States government did not want European powers returning to the New World. England distrusted Spain's ally, France, and she wanted to keep trading with the new South American republics. Britain approached the United States, suggesting they issue a joint proclamation to oppose Spanish intervention in the New World.

Once again, the short, well-dressed Secretary of State addressed the cabinet. "A joint decree with England won't help us," he maintained. "In fact, I believe it will hurt us. England's worried about France. We're concerned about Russia's designs on Oregon." Adams paused to clear his throat. "We must stay free of entanglement with England. If we don't, we'll be like a small rowboat following in the wake of a British man-of-war.

"We must adopt our own policy. We should issue a proclamation declaring that America and Europe stay out of one another's affairs." Adams' high-pitched voice rose with excitement. "Gentlemen, we must let Europe know that we consider any move by any country to control an independent state in the New World as unfriendly toward the United States."

The Monroe Doctrine announced to all nations that the New World would resist all foreign intervention from that point on. God was preserving His grand plan. Through the efforts of John Quincy Adams, He was moving America to a place of global independence.

But the greatest hurdle of all to overcome still remained. By the 1820s the country was trembling as it picked its way through the lion's den of slavery. What would become of God's New Israel now?

CHAPTER
TEN

Any kingdom divided against itself is laid waste; and any city or house divided against itself shall not stand. (Matthew 12:25)

A HOUSE DIVIDING

The wake-up horn sounded, and the six men and four women in cabin fourteen rolled off their straw pallets, groaning. They groped in the darkness for their field clothes. Those who still had shoes fumbled around the floor in search of them. The women grabbed some hoecakes and filled drinking gourds with water. Another day of sweat and toil had begun.

Streaks of pink and gray lined the eastern sky as the last man dashed toward the field. Frantically, he tucked in the shirt he had been slow to find. The overseer waited, slapping the handle of his whip in the palm of his hand.

"Jethro," he said wearily, "you're late again. Step forward."

The slave did as he was told. The overseer lashed him twelve times as the boy hollered and the others watched. He would not be late again, anytime soon.

This same scene repeated itself throughout the deep south. Before dawn, thousands of slaves awoke to face days of hard labor for their white masters. Many sweated in the cotton fields. Others worked as house slaves. One fifteen-minute break for lunch punctuated their long, hot day. At day's end during the fall, the field hands lifted the bales of cotton over their heads and wearily walked to the gin to have the cotton weighed. They worried about not making their quota, the daily amount of cotton each slave was to pick. Beatings often followed for those who failed to measure up.

Poverty defined the life of a slave in the nineteenth century. Often seven to twelve of them, from different families, were crammed into clapboard shanties with no windows or floors. There was little protection from sweltering heat in summer or nipping cold in winter. A pair of pants and a couple of shirts clothed a male slave in summer. In winter, he received a pair of shoes, a jacket, a blanket, and two caps. A quart of cornmeal and a piece of pork comprised his daily food. An Englishman estimated that the cost for all of this was one pound, ten shillings per year. Yet a slave's labor was valued at twenty pounds per year. A slave received barely one-tenth of what he deserved.

Why did the institution of slavery prosper during the nineteenth century in America? For one thing, the south's mild climate and rich soil encouraged plantation farming. Southerners harvested thousands of acres of tobacco, cotton, rice, indigo, and hemp. These plantations required field hands, and slave labor fit the need perfectly, especially because it was so cheap. Once a landowner had regained his initial purchase price for a slave, he could enjoy his profits. By 1790, the states of Maryland, Virginia, the Carolinas, and Georgia reported almost 650,000 slaves within their borders. Slavery was rapidly taking hold in the South.

Then, in 1793, a single incident sealed the south's fate. Eli Whitney, a young Yale graduate, sailed to Savannah to tutor the children of a prominent family. On the trip, he met Catherine Greene, a Georgia farm widow. When Whitney's position fell through, Mrs. Greene invited him to Mulberry Grove, her rice plantation. The young northerner accepted.

One evening, a group of gentlemen visited Mulberry Grove and relaxed on the veranda. A long, dirt driveway circled up to the squared, white mansion with its Greek columns and manicured lawn. Massive oaks draped with moss lined the road.

"This has been a good growing season for cotton," one gentleman commented, lighting his pipe and leaning against a huge pillar.

"But we won't make a profit," moaned another. "How can we? Takes too long to separate the seeds by hand. I tell you, we need a gin!"

"Upland cotton's a good product," Phineas Miller chimed in. "And England now has the mills to process all the raw cotton we can send her. She pays top dollar too. We've got to find a way to gin it!" Miller spotted Whitney, seated on the top step. "Eli, you like to tinker. Why don't you give it a try?"

"I'm afraid I haven't the tools or the necessary equipment," he replied. "And it would take quite a bit of capital to get 'em."

"I might be able to help," Miller offered. "What if I purchase the equipment and you develop the machine? We'll enter a partnership."

Whitney agreed. By early '93, he had developed a working model. A hand-cranked cylinder thrust thin wire spikes down through metal slots into raw cotton. As this cylinder turned, the spikes raked the cotton, bringing up cotton lint but no seeds. The seeds were too thick to pass through the narrow slots. A second rotating cylinder, mounted with brushes, combed the lint from the tips of the spikes.

Whitney's gin revolutionized the cotton industry in the south. The warm rich soil along the Gulf Coast beckoned cotton growers. And these landowners needed cheap labor, so they bought more slaves. Slavery had rooted itself firmly and deeply in southern soil.

On a warm March morning in 1820, a line of slaves shuffled along a dirt road in the nation's capital. Small clouds of dust floated into the air as their chinking chains beat time with their movement. Six males led the column, shackled to each other by their necks and wrists. Four females and four small children trailed behind under the watchful eye of the black driver and his long switch. In back of them all, on a horse, rode the white trader, wearing two long-handled pistols in his belt and holding a loosely coiled blacksnake whip in his right hand.

The slaves moved slowly, with heavy hearts and sad faces. Each one had his own story to tell. The leader was a tall black who had been part of an illegal shipment of slaves, smuggled ashore north of Norfolk. The two men behind him were brothers, born and raised on a tobacco plantation outside Roanoke. When the plantation fell on hard times, their weeping owner had to sell them, forcing the young men to leave the only family and friends they had ever known. Next in line walked two troublemakers. The first had already lost an ear, probably from stealing or striking an overseer. The other knew how to read and write, a sure sign of trouble. He might read a newspaper, discover the growing arguments against slavery, and get ideas about freedom.

The last man and first woman in the column were two "house niggers" from Alexandria, Virginia trained in household duties. As husband and wife, they hoped to be sold together with their two children. But the chances of this were slim. The slaves had observed the trader since leaving Alexandria. He would say anything to make a sale. If he could get more by separating them, then he would separate them, and they would never see one another again. Only God could help them.

On they trudged. Just ahead on the left stood the Capitol building with its endless white steps. In a minute they would pass by. Wanting to make a good impression, the trader muttered something to the driver.

"Sing, you slaves!" the driver ordered.

The slaves muddled on. The driver then popped his switch. Immediately, the men and women started humming and singing. Their mournful tune rose to the heavens. Although no one could understand the words, the meaning was clear. Their song described the horror of families torn apart and of loved ones tortured and beaten. It depicted a people who had lost their dignity as well as their hope. It spoke of death and the release that comes only when a person goes home to be with the Lord.

As the group neared the gleaming steps of the Capitol, their anguished faces bent low, toward the ground. They did not notice the Congressmen in their brocaded waistcoats, out taking the air during a recess. They did not see the elegant ladies of fashion who had packed the visitors' gallery. But the Congressmen and ladies noticed the slaves. All conversation died away, as the despairing sound of their voices filled the morning air.

Suddenly, the sergeant-at-arms rang his handbell to summon the Congressmen back inside. Spectators crowded the House gallery. Journalists fumbled with their papers preparing to take notes. An important question was before the House of Representatives.

Should the Missouri Territory be admitted into the Union as a slave state or a free state? This was the question, and it was by far the hottest issue facing Congress in its thirty-three years of existence. Since the majority of settlers in Missouri were slaveholders, the area's application for statehood contained no clause restricting slavery. But admitting another slave state would upset the balance of power in the Senate. And northerners did not want that.

James Tallmadge, Jr., of New York, introduced an amendment to the application. "I move we admit Missouri but prohibit any more slaves from coming into the state from now on. I also move we grant freedom to children born to these slaves after they've reached the age of 25."

Slaveholding states strenuously protested. Congress

should not have the power to dictate whether or not a state could maintain its slave status. And the southerners certainly were not going to tilt the balance of power in the Senate by admitting another free state.

John Scott from Missouri spoke up. "We have the right to be admitted as a slaveholding state."

Thomas Cobb of Georgia jumped to his feet. "If those who wish to restrict slavery persist," he exclaimed, "the Union will dissolve." Cobb then pointed his finger at Tallmadge, who had proposed the amendment. "You have kindled a fire which all the waters of the ocean cannot put out!"

The Speaker of the House, Henry Clay, gaveled for order. Tallmadge spoke up. "If slavery extends across the west, you'll place a vulture on your own heart." Tallmadge paused. He then looked up at the gallery. "No," he declared, "you'll place a dagger in the hands of the slaves themselves!"

The House grew absolutely still. Tallmadge had touched a deep nerve. Would the slaves revolt? Tallmadge continued, pointing to the tall windows circling the House chamber.

"A slave driver has just passed the door of your Capitol," he bellowed. "He was driving about fifteen of these wretched victims of his power. The males, who might raise the arm of vengeance, were handcuffed and chained to each other. The females and children marched in the rear, under the driver's whip." Tallmadge fixed his gaze on the speaker. "Yes, sir, such a scene has been witnessed from the windows of Congress Hall by those of us who are members of the legislative council of the Republic of America!"

Selma Hale, Congressman from New Hampshire, later wrote about the Missouri debates that day. "It was a painful scene. I hope a similar discussion will never again take place in our walls."

Over the next few months, hearts hardened on both sides. When Congress adjourned for a summer recess, it had not reached a solution. And the summer recess did not cool the hot tempers either. The lawmakers returned to Washington more determined than ever to keep their regional stands. The north and the south could not agree.

Observers wondered aloud whether this was the beginning of the end of the United States of America. Those who loved the republic enough to put her interests first felt a deep sadness at what was taking place. Finally, a few key men who held the vision of one nation under God, worked out a compromise.

"If you accept Missouri as a slave state, the south will admit Maine as a free state." Speaker Henry Clay addressed his northern colleagues. "The south will also agree to forbid slavery in the rest of the Louisiana Purchase."

The north agreed, and Congress struck the Missouri Compromise. Neither side was truly happy with the result, but the representatives felt they could live with it. The country sighed with relief. Just as it had done in 1787 during the Constitutional Convention, Congress had once again saved the peace, at least for a while.

But the issues surrounding slavery would not die. John Quincy Adams wrote, "Slavery hangs over this country like a black cloud." And black it was. Just 40 years later, 600,000 men would give their lives to find a solution. And the nation would be pulled apart, barely 87 years after its birth.

Slavery was truly a national tragedy. It hurt not only the lives of those whose skin was black but also the lives of those whose skin was white. As a Christian people, we must look into the very heart of our past sins and learn from them, so we will never be doomed to repeat them.

CHAPTER
ELEVEN

Woe to him who builds his house without righteousness and his upper rooms without justice, Who uses his neighbor's services without pay and does not give him his wages. (Jeremiah 22:13)

A FIRE BELL IN THE NIGHT

The black whip whistled through the air and lashed the girl's body. The overseer dealt more blows. After four lashes, the slave girl trembled. The overseer glanced to his left, at the other slaves assembled to witness the punishment. The girl's brother stood with his hands clenched into fists at his side. If only he could do something, anything. But he could not. The overseer would like nothing better than to shoot him. So the brother stood there, shaking, as the whip hissed its horrifying sound.

Nine strokes fell. Now the slave girl screamed for mercy, begging her brother to help. Tears streamed down his face. The overseer watched him closely, aiming another lash at his sister. The brother could stand it no longer. With a bloodcurdling scream, he lunged forward. Fortunately, the mistress of the plantation saved them both by waving the overseer to stop. It was over at last.

What causes one man to hold another against his will? The answer rests deep within the fallen nature of man.

God's Word clearly states that "all have sinned and fall(en) short of the glory of God" (Romans 3:23). Without Christ, a person's sinful nature poisons even good intentions and leads a person to behave with cruelty toward his fellowman, especially when the latter is defenseless. This is exactly what happened in slaveholding regions during the nineteenth century.

The rift between the north and the south reflected a fundamental difference between the two regions. The Puritan heritage of the north taught that all men were created equal in the sight of God, regardless of color. Work hard and get ahead and help those less fortunate than yourself. This was the Puritan way. But in the south, it was different. The aristocratic traditions of its landowners wove a class-conscious society. Slaves were nothing more than property. Not only did the south need slaves to toil in its fields, it required them to maintain its class structure, perpetuating the myth that all men are not truly equal in God's sight.

Yet, many southerners acknowledged the evils of slavery. And some of them, like Methodist minister Jeremiah Jeter, treated their slaves with kindness and respect. Jeter even yearned to free his people, but obstacles blocked him at every turn. The law in his state of Virginia prohibited the manumission, or release, of slaves. With family members on nearby plantations, most of the slaves did not want to leave anyway. They begged the minister to keep them. How were they going to support themselves if he did release them? Nobody in Eastern Virginia would hire freed slaves. Surely Jeter could not transport the blacks back to Africa. Most had been born in America and would die from the voyage or the change. No, the loving, Christian thing to do was to keep them.

Unfortunately, not every Christian held the same compassionate heart. And here lies one of the greatest tragedies of slavery. A personal relationship with Christ did not guarantee that the person would not fall prey to the system. Many Christian slave owners actually believed that God had placed whites in authority and ordained blacks to serve them. Of course, this meant they must diligently keep the blacks in line. And so, even Christians sometimes did things to slaves that Christ would not have approved, let alone ever done Himself.

The system itself was evil, and it brought out the worst in otherwise good people. Angelina Grimké, the daughter of a South Carolina Supreme Court Justice, wrote about a Christian acquaintance in Charleston.

> This woman donated to charities. She visited the poor. In fact, she gave more money than just about anyone. But she beat her slaves, often for no reason at all. She used small paddles called 'pancake sticks', which she kept at convenient places around the house. Frequently, she ordered a brother to whip his sister or a sister to lash her brother. The room she used to inflict this torture was the very place she used to pray and hold her prayer meetings.

Christian leaders such as Francis Asbury and Peter Cartwright spoke out against slavery. They even spearheaded an effort to evangelize both blacks and whites in the south. But many slave owners did not want to promote Christianity, fearing slaves might get the idea they were "as good as white folks."

Nonetheless, many slaves *did* know Jesus, and this faith sustained them. Despite all the suffering, they never lost hope that somehow, someday, the Lord would deliver them from bondage like the Israelites in Egypt. The black Church moved underground. Slaves developed codes to announce a prayer gathering and met secretly at night in the woods. They prayed, they sang, and they worshiped the Lord. He was the only One they could trust. And amazingly, most of them kept on trusting, no matter what happened to them.

Sometimes this trust brought punishment. One slave named Thomas Jones hungered for salvation and prayed to his Savior often. One day, his master discovered Thomas had attended a prayer meeting.

"I told you I'd whip you if you went to one of those meetings!" the master yelled. "Didn't I tell you to stop this foolish praying? There's no such thing as heaven and hell. These Christians are nothing but hypocrites."

"Master," Thomas replied. "I can't help myself. I want to go to heaven when I die."

In a rage, the master stripped Thomas and whipped him, tearing his back open in a dozen places. "Now, will you stop this praying?"

"No, sir," Thomas replied, "can't stop prayin'."

"Then, I'll whip you to death!"

The master lashed the slave a second time. Then he cast down the bloody cowhide and exclaimed, "If you're going be a fool, then be one."

The whipping did not stop Thomas. At the next prayer meeting, he accepted Jesus and received salvation. He later wrote:

I felt the glory of God's love warming my heart and making me happy. I shouted aloud, wanting to tell my poor slave brothers and sisters what a dear Savior I had found. Binney Pennison asked me if I could forgive my master. I told him I could, and that I'd pray for God to forgive him, too. Binney asked me what I'd do if my master whipped me again when he found out. I told him I'd ask Jesus to help me bear the pain and to forgive my master for being so wicked.

Jones told his master the next morning. Down came the cowhide from its place on the wall. With a sigh, the slave began to remove his clothing.

"You crazy fool!" his master screamed. "You keep your clothes on till I tell you to take them off!"

With that, he proceeded to whip Thomas over his jacket. The slave enjoyed such peace of mind in the Lord, that he scarcely felt the cowhide. And that was the last beating he ever received.

Thomas had been beaten for righteousness' sake. His story had a happy ending. But not every story ended this well. Sarah Grimké, the sister of Angelina, recounted an incident told to her by a close friend whose husband was a wealthy plantation owner.

On a nearby plantation, a planter was dining with a slave owner. The planter remarked that religion among slaves was nothing more than hypocrisy. The owner replied. "That's not true. I have a slave who I believe would rather die than deny his Savior." The planter ridiculed the owner, daring him to prove it. The owner called the slave and ordered him to deny his faith. When the slave refused, the owner whipped him mercilessly until he died. The slave never denied the Lord and, that day, became a martyr for Jesus.

The hideous thing about absolute power is that the people possessing it do not realize what effect it is having on their own souls. Slavery hardened the hearts of these slave owners, robbing them of compassion. They thought of these human beings as nothing more than property. Slaves could be whipped. They could be killed. They could be bought and sold without regard to family ties. They were no better than cows.

Josiah Henson was five years old when his master suddenly died. The estate, including the slaves, was sold at public auction. The slaves stood on the auctioneer's stand. Josiah and his family trembled as the buyers pawed them, looking into their mouths and feeling their muscles. Josiah later recounted what happened as the auction began.

> My brothers and sisters were bid off first, one by one. My mother, paralyzed by grief, clutched me by the hand. Her turn came, and she was bought by Isaac Riley of Montgomery County in Maryland. Then, it was my turn. While the bidding for me was going on, my mother frantically pushed through the crowd to her new master. Falling at his feet, she clung to his knees and pleaded, "Master, master, please buy my baby. Please spare me one of my little ones!" The man pulled himself away and kicked her so violently that she had to creep away. As she crawled off, I heard her sob out. "Oh, Lord Jesus, how long, how long shall I suffer this way?"

Suffering and torment were their daily companions.

Often, their suffering led to death. Sarah Grimké visited a plantation in North Carolina, where the master and mistress were well known for their hospitality.

While walking one chilly winter day, Sarah discovered an old, white-haired slave lying alone in a windy shack on the property. The man lay on a bed of boards and had a gaping, untreated sore in his side. Sarah asked him about this. The slave told her that he had no one to care for him. The other slaves tried to fetch him something to eat so he would not starve, but he was dying. Sarah related that the master of this plantation later became governor of the state of North Carolina.

Slavery locked both sides into a no-win situation. It bound the whites just as tightly as it did the blacks. The south needed its slaves. It was as simple as that. Southerners might argue against slavery and talk of "gradual emancipation," the idea of gradually releasing the slaves. But the talk was cheap. Even if they wanted to, southerners could not let their slaves go. It would mean financial disaster. A plantation owner's entire wealth was tied up in his slaves. Most slaveholders believed that emancipating slaves meant destroying the south. No, they argued, everyone must try to live within the system and make the best of it.

But what if the slaves rebelled? Southern states passed strict laws to crush any thoughts of rebellion. They forbid blacks to congregate without a white present. Patrols combed the areas at night, making sure blacks stayed in their cabins. Rumors of conspiracies spread like a plague. Everyone remembered what had happened in South

Carolina in 1739, and they did not want it to happen again. Just outside Charleston, some slaves had revolted, killing two warehouse guards and stealing some rifles. On their armed march to Florida, other blacks had joined in. The swelling force had killed every white in its path. And this Cato Conspiracy engraved itself in the south's memory forever.

Fear dominated southern life, and much of this fear grew out of guilt. Whether they acknowledged it or not, many southerners still felt some pain about what was taking place. In Louisiana, a white woman named Kate Stone asserted, "Always I felt the moral guilt of it, how impossible it must be for an owner of slaves to win his way to heaven." In Virginia, Anne Meade Page, a devout slave owner, lamented. "The evils of slavery cannot be seen by human powers. They form a part of those hidden things of darkness . . . linked by a chain that reaches into the dominion of Satan, not only here on earth, but into his more complete dominion in the realms of deepest hell."

Fear and guilt tormented many slave owners but often did not surface until they approached death's door. Scores of deathbed testimonies recounted the terror of dying plantation owners begging for forgiveness.

Thomas Stevens, a slave owner, suffered from seizures. One of his slaves, John Brown, recorded what happened as the master lay dying.

> In his fright, he sent for us and asked us to forgive him. I remember his calling old Aunt Sally and begging and praying for her to get the devil away from behind the door. It's a common belief among us that all the masters die in an awful fright. We

think that their minds must be dreadful uneasy about holding slaves.

Daniel Webster wisely advised his northern brethren to assure the south that they considered slavery as a calamity and not a crime. Webster urged the north to share the south's burden of putting an end to it. Had this inspired attitude caught on, the nation might have avoided disaster. But few northerners agreed with Webster. They were not about to compensate southern slave holders for their financial losses. The northern attitude rang ominously loud. "It's their problem; let them deal with it."

Profoundly troubled by the passions stirred by the Missouri question, Thomas Jefferson called the rising controversy a "fire bell in the night," awakening him and filling him with dread. "It is hushed, indeed, for the moment," Jefferson wrote. "But this is a reprieve only, not a final sentence . . . . We have a wolf by the ears, and we can neither hold him, nor safely let him go." To Jefferson, the Missouri question had inflamed public opinion to such a degree that he was afraid the Union would eventually break apart.

And he was right. Northerners adamantly opposed slavery. Southerners had to support it. No single incident, short of war, would reconcile the two sides. But it was not yet time for the collision. As the country rumbled down the track toward war, the Almighty placed a beloved leader at the engine's throttle, to raise the banner of a united America. His name was Andrew Jackson.

CHAPTER
TWELVE

For even as the body is one and yet has many members, and all the members of the body, though they are many, are one body. (1 Corinthians 12:12)

LIBERTY AND UNION FOREVER

Despite the growing conflict over slavery, God continued to shed His grace on America. In the 1830s, He raised up another leader to carry the torch of national unity, Andrew Jackson. The events that brought Old Hickory to the White House chiseled his character into the determined man everyone loved so dearly. And it also taught him the importance of the Union as one nation under God.

On a quiet morning in May 1806, three men waited by their horses in a foggy glade near Nashville, Tennessee. Charles Dickinson glanced at the treetops and tugged at his leather gloves. A faint smile crossed his lips as he straightened his light blue jacket. Today was the day of the duel. Everything was set, and Dickinson felt confident.

Three horsemen trotted toward them at a slow, deliberate pace with a young Andrew Jackson leading the small party. As they approached, Jackson leaned over to his friend, John Overton. "He's sure to fire first," Jackson confided. "The chances are nine out of ten he'll hit me. But that won't matter." Jackson grasped the reins as he neared the glade. "I'll take my time, aim deliberately, and kill him, if it's the last thing I do. No one slurs my wife, not my Rachel."

Jackson's group arrived and dismounted. The two parties greeted one another. In the middle of the clearing, some aides drove two stakes into the ground, exactly 24 feet apart. The two duelists would soon stand at these stakes, facing each other with their loaded pistols pointed straight down. At the command to fire, they would take aim and shoot. Dickinson stepped confidently to his mark. The tall Jackson, clad in a bulky, loose-fitting frock coat, walked over to his.

"Gentlemen," Overton called out. "Are you ready?"

"Yes," responded Dickinson.

"Yes," replied Jackson.

"Fire!"

At the command, Dickinson quickly raised his gun and fired. A puff of smoke rose from Jackson's coat, just to the left of his center button. His lean body shuddered, and his left arm flew to his chest. Then, he straightened and, slowly raised his pistol.

Dumbfounded, Dickinson stepped backward. "My God!" he screeched, "have I missed him?"

"Back to the mark, sir!" Overton ordered.

Dickinson returned to the stake and folded his arms across his chest. He watched Jackson take careful aim. Slowly, Jackson exerted pressure on the hair trigger, and a second shot broke the silence. The ball tore through Dickinson's side, just below his folded arms. He toppled forward, blood gushing from his wound. The surgeon rushed over to him, but little could be done. He was dead.

Jackson turned and walked away stiffly. Overton noticed that his friend's left shoe was full of blood. Shocked, he and the surgeon eased Jackson to the ground and gently removed his coat. Jackson had been hit. The bullet had broken two ribs and was embedded in his chest cavity.

"Andy, it looks like this old coat of yours saved your life," Overton commented. "Otherwise, Dickinson's bullet would have hit your heart."

"I'd have hit him, if he'd shot me through the brain!" Jackson answered through clenched teeth.

Jackson paid a severe price for that victory. Doctors could not remove the bullet because it lay too close to the heart. He carried it with him for the rest of his life. Because it lodged against his left lung, a pulmonary abscess formed. Over the years, Jackson suffered one respiratory infection after another, causing constant coughing. But that was not all. Throughout his later years, Jackson suffered from many different ailments. Dysentery, malaria, rheumatism, and severe toothaches plagued him. They robbed him of sleep and tormented him to the point a normal man would have longed for death. But Jackson was not just a normal man. And self-pity was not part of his character. With the iron will of a bulldog, he endured whatever came his way. And this trait endeared him to many, making him a legend in his own time.

Jackson's journey to the White House almost ended after he captured Florida for the United States in 1818. The general returned to his beloved farm near Nashville,

Tennessee, where he planned to retire from public life. But friends and supporters would not hear of it. They elected him to the United States Senate and, in 1824, urged him to run for President.

In the election of 1824, the popular vote went to Jackson, with 153,000 votes and support from every region except New England. New Englander John Quincy Adams won 114,000 votes. The other two contenders, Speaker of the House Henry Clay and Secretary of the Treasury William Crawford received 47,000 votes each. With no clear electoral majority, the decision fell into the lap of the House of Representatives. The House had to choose from the top three contenders.

This eliminated Kentucky's Henry Clay from the race. Jealous of Jackson's fame, Clay threw his backing to Adams. He instructed his Kentucky colleagues in the House to support Adams. And they did, ignoring the fact that Adams had not received a single vote in Kentucky, and the state legislature had just instructed them to vote for Jackson. The delegates from New York, Ohio, and Louisiana tilted the scale, giving Adams the majority he needed to become the sixth President of the United States.

It was not God's timing for Jackson to complete his trek to the presidency. In spite of his popularity, Jackson's vision for the country still focused on regional needs. He had not clearly understood the idea of one nation under God. He also still had too many political enemies in Washington, who would undermine his effectiveness as President.

Enraged, Jackson and his supporters prepared themselves for the election of 1828. This time victory would not be snatched from their hands. The good of the country was at stake. During the four years of waiting, Jackson gave much thought to what the Union could and should become. He read newspapers from across the land. And his hatred of the politicians who were taking advantage of the common folk was distilled into a nationwide call for reform.

"The administration of the government has stained our national character," he wrote his friend John Coffee. "It rests with the people to work it out."

Planning and fuming and waiting, the general shaped a national reform policy. By the time of the campaign of 1828, he no longer had the outlook of a Tennessee general. The scope of his vision had expanded to include the whole nation, from Maine to Florida to Missouri. Most important of all, he no longer saw three distinct regions. He envisioned one big country. And this was the country he passionately wanted to serve.

In the late winter of 1829, a lone man paused at the top of a mountain pass to gaze at the late afternoon sun. The mountains and foothills to the west seemed bathed in a golden haze. Above, a hawk circled in the clear sky. Far below, a deer and her fawn timidly approached a pond in a wooded valley. The man on foot shifted his old army pack and started down the eastern slope when a movement caught his eye. Coming up the winding track was a farm wagon pulled by two horses. Exhausted from his travels, the old walker plunked down on a rock.

As the wagon reached the top of the pass, the farmer at the reins called out, "You going to see Old Hickory get sworn in?"

The walker grinned. "Sure am."

"Well, so are we. Climb aboard!"

That night, the group joined the campfire of two other wagons headed for Washington. All over eastern America, the scene was the same. It was almost as if someone had announced a national camp meeting. Farmers, river men, hired hands, and freed slaves swarmed on the nation's capital. Some had fought with Jackson in New Orleans or Florida. Most had never laid eyes on him. Yet, that did not matter. They liked what they had read and heard. And most of all, they just plain liked him. Yep, Andy Jackson was their man, the people's President. The fifty-three year reign of the eastern aristocrats had finally come to an end.

The morning of March 4, 1828, dawned bright and clear. Over 20,000 people gathered on the mall below the Capitol. Washington society had never seen anything like it. Daniel Webster commented, "I never saw such a crowd here before. They really seem to think the country is rescued from some dreadful danger."

The crowd squinted in the sunlight and waited. When the tall, gaunt figure emerged between the high columns of the Capitol, a thunderous roar arose from the multitude. Thousands of hats came off, hands waved, and faces beamed with delight. As Jackson concluded his brief inauguration speech, he bowed to the people. Cheers rose to the heavens. The new President was showing them just what they wanted to see. America was their country, and he was their servant.

A short while later, Andrew Jackson leaned against the curtained window of his lodging to watch the festivities at the White House across the street. He had left early to avoid the mobs. Despite the gaiety, however, his heart was sad. Tomorrow he would move over there, but it would be without the woman he loved. Rachel had died of a massive heart attack right after the election. He grieved for her now. Touching the velvet curtain with his hands, Jackson reflected on Rachel's funeral last Christmas Eve. Ten thousand people had crowded around the Hermitage that cold, wet day to pay their respects. Everyone had loved her. He still loved her, and now he faced life without her.

The weary man turned and walked away from the window. He was not a quitter, though. His country needed him. Each day, more issues wedged the regions further apart. Some folks were saying the Union wouldn't last five more years. Jackson slumped down on the big four poster bed. *No*, he resolved, *the Union will not dissolve while I am President.*

But the strength of the Union would be tested sooner than he anticipated. Two issues before Congress threatened unity. In 1828, Congress passed a tariff known as the Tariff of Abominations. Following the War of 1813, Europe had flooded the American market with cheap, European products. This bill taxed those imported goods. The industrial north supported the measure but the agricultural south did not. The south depended on imported foreign products.

"This tariff is unconstitutional!" they protested. "It protects the economy of one section at the expense of the other! It isn't intended to raise revenue at all. It's meant to hurt the south."

South Carolina went further. Led by John Calhoun, the state developed a policy to deal with the tariffs. "The Constitution is a compact made by the states. A state legislature can declare null and void any federal statute that hurts the vital interest of that state." South Carolina determined to resist the new tariffs.

Meanwhile, a second issue stirred the boiling pot of division between the two regions. In 1829, Senator Samuel Foot of Connecticut proposed that Congress shut down the sale of public land. Cotton growers were pouring into the Louisiana Territory, buying fresh land for growing cotton. This worried the north. It meant that even more slave states would join the Union and upset the balance of power in Congress. Debates over Foot's bill consumed the Senate.

One of the south's finest debaters, Robert Hayne of South Carolina, rose to his feet. "I agree with Mr. Benton from Missouri," he stated. "The north wants to hold its citizens captive and condemn them to miserable lives in New England sweatshops. But the south and west believe in America as a land of opportunity. We want people to expand their horizons. There's no reason to stop the sale of public land."

As Hayne spoke, Daniel Webster walked by the Senate chamber. At the time, the Senator from Massachusetts was arguing a case before the Supreme Court. But the Court had adjourned early that chilly afternoon. Webster decided to step in. He quickly realized that the Senator from South Carolina had launched a deliberate attacked on New England. This was far more serious than a debate over the sale of public land. The south wanted to forge an alliance with the west against the north.

An alarmed Webster listened. Hayne attacked the whole "American system" of roads and canals. "What possible interest could South Carolina have in a canal in Ohio?" he asked. His magnificent speech captured the ears of everyone as he argued in favor of states' rights. And the preservation of the Union balanced precariously on the cliff of his convincing words. Daniel Webster knew what he had to do.

On the final day of the debate, a throng of spectators packed the chamber. Practically everyone who was anyone in Washington had come to hear Webster,the great orator from New England, defend the Union. Even representatives from the House had slipped in to listen. A hush fell over the assembly as the Senator rose to his feet. He began by addressing Senator Hayne.

> Sir, we narrow-minded New Englanders do not reason as you do. We look upon the States, not as separated, but as united, under one government.
> I don't agree that the states have a constitutional right to interfere with a law of Congress. The people forged the national government, and they mean for it to endure. Your policy of states' rights and nullification will bring an end to this Union.

After speaking for a long time, Webster paused. Then he pointed to the American flag hanging in the Senate chamber. "Behold this gorgeous ensign," he majestically ended his speech. "It is known and honored throughout the earth. And it bears those words held dear to every true American heart—Liberty and Union, now and forever, one and inseparable!"

Webster gathered his notes and sat down. His words echoed through the chamber. No one clapped. Everyone sat still, as if in a trance. Finally, the speaker's gavel broke the long silence.

The debate between Hayne and Webster dealt a staggering blow to the supporters of states' rights and nullification. But they still had an ace up their sleeve, or so they thought. Andrew Jackson had not taken a stand. Surely they count count on Old Hickory, the champion of the people. He would throw his weight against the eastern industrialists. On April 13, these supporters planned a dinner honoring the birthday of Thomas Jefferson. They invited President Jackson, his cabinet, and noted political figures from each of the 24 states.

The grand evening arrived. In those days, dinner party toasts were a well-planned event. Men would stand and give toasts in careful order. As each state's spokesman made his toast, the President realized what was happening. The toasts reflected a full scale support of states' rights. Some of them amounted to treason. Jackson masked his anger as shrewdly as the expert card player he was. When his turn came, the President stood up. Raising his glass in the air, he declared, "Our Federal Union. It must be preserved!"

For a moment, no one moved. Then, all eyes riveted on Vice President John Calhoun, the next in line to toast. Calhoun was a strong advocate of states' rights. What would he say? Slowly, the Vice President pushed back his chair and rose to his feet. The contents of his glass spilled over the rim as his hands trembled. Calhoun swallowed. "The Union, next to our liberties, most dear."

News of Jackson's toast swept the nation. Jackson supported the Union! A short while later, a South Carolina Congressman asked if the President would like to send a message to his friends in South Carolina. "Tell them for me," Old Hickory scowled, "that they can talk and write resolutions and print threats to their hearts' content. But if one drop of blood is shed in defiance of the laws of the United States, I'll hang the first man I can get my hands on to the first tree I can find."

By 1832, the fabric holding the nation together was tearing apart at the seams. But John Quincy Adams, who had left the White House deeply hurt, discovered that God was not finished with him yet. Friends urged Adams to run for Congress, and he did, winning by a wide margin. Feeling younger than he had in years, Adams rolled up his sleeves and got to work replacing the hated Tariff of Abominations.

However, nullification was not like a snowball rolling downhill gathering speed and size. On November 24, 1832, the legislature of South Carolina declared the tariff acts null and void and threatened secession if the federal government tried to collect the tax. Jackson fired back a reply. "Disunion by armed force is treason. Don't do anything so horrible! To say that any State may secede from the Union is to say that the United States is not a nation."

When Jackson submitted a bill to Congress permitting him to enforce the tax, Congress debated the Force Bill.

John Calhoun and the delegation from South Carolina were enraged. The former Vice President stood in front of his colleagues, his unruly hair wet with perspiration. His deep-set eyes glared at the chamber, and the jaw muscles on his chiseled features tensed.

"Southerners," he screeched, "you must stand with us and be counted for the southern cause!"

Once again, Daniel Webster spoke up for the Union. "Giving states the right to declare a federal law null and void strikes a deadly blow at our nation," he pronounced. "To say it won't dismember the Union is like believing you can plunge over Niagara Falls and stop halfway down." Webster halted, eyeing Calhoun. "Sir, to the world, it must seem incredible that a single state should rush into conflict with the rest and destroy the world's last hope."

Webster's words hit the mark. The gallery erupted in a thunderous, sustained applause. Calhoun and his supporters stalked out of the chamber. The Force Bill passed 32 to 1.

In the end, South Carolina realized it stood alone. No other southern state elected to stand with her. South Carolina could not withstand federal troops by itself so the state rescinded its nullification law. And, for the moment at least, the crisis had passed.

God was preserving His plan through three great national leaders. John Marshall headed the Supreme Court through the tidal wave of Jefferson's stormy attempts to weaken the federal government. Andrew Jackson's courage sheltered the Union from those calling for secession. And Daniel Webster's impassioned speeches raised the flag of patriotism and pride. But these were not the only men carrying the torch for a strong union. God had someone else waiting in the wings.

CHAPTER
THIRTEEN

Go into all the world and preach the gospel to all creation. (Mark 16:15)

A LIGHTNING STORM OF REVIVAL

 Adams, New York, was beautiful in the fall of 1821. Located in the Adirondack Mountains just east of Lake Ontario, the area offered a peaceful settlement to New England pioneers heading west during the 1800s. It was October, and the air was chilly. The early morning sun fired the trees a brilliant red and gold.

North of the village and over a hill lay a wood. The young lawyer walked out of his office and turned toward it. "I'll give my heart to God before I come down from that hill," he declared aloud as he hiked along the dirt path. The tall man followed the path, enjoying the beauty of the goldenrod growing along the sides. A woodchuck ambled in front of him just as some Canadian geese squawked overhead. He glanced up but did not really see them. He was deep in prayer:

I've been reading the Bible for some time now, Lord, Your Word says I don't need my own righteousness to get to heaven, but that's not what I've been taught. Some ministers say I can do nothing to bring about my own salvation, that the best I can do is just to hope You will save me.

The rugged New Yorker stopped and gazed at a brilliant red maple leaf. Then he looked up at the light blue sky with its white, wispy clouds and marveled at God's creation. "Lord," he muttered, "I'm twenty-nine years old, and I must make my peace with you. It must be here, today." The man started walking again, his thoughts focused on Christ. *Almighty God, You sent Your Son to die on the cross for my sins. It's time for me to settle the question of my soul's salvation.*

Charles Finney reached the crest of the hill. He tried to pray but thought he heard leaves rustling. He quickly glanced around to see if anyone was there. Seeing no one, Finney tried to pray again. And again, he thought he heard someone moving in the brush. In despair, the lawyer sobbed, "This is nothing but my own pride. Here I am on my knees, confessing to the great and Holy God, and ashamed for anyone to find me!" With that, the six-foot-two-inch man crumbled to his knees and wept.

Suddenly, a Scripture verse came to his mind. "Then you will call upon Me and come and pray to Me, and I will listen to you. And you will seek Me and find Me, when you search for Me with all your heart" (Jeremiah 29:12–13). Finney realized this was God's voice to him, directing him to believe with his heart. More promises came to his mind.

The man prayed all afternoon and lost track of the time. Finally he noticed that the trees were making long shadows and a slight wind chilled the air. He got up and hiked back to the village.

That evening, he returned to his office and built a fire. While playing his bass violin and singing, the young lawyer began to cry. He rushed into the back room to pray, when suddenly a strange thing happened.

> As I went in and shut the door after me, it seemed as if I met the Lord Jesus Christ face to face. I saw him as I would see any other man. He said nothing, but looked at me in such a manner as to break me right down at his feet. I fell down at His feet and poured out my soul to him. I wept aloud like a child.

After the vision faded, Finney walked back to the front office. The fire had nearly burned out. Sitting beside the dying embers, the young man reflected on what had just occurred, but there was more to come.

> The Holy Spirit descended upon me . . . like a wave of electricity. It seemed like the very breath of God. No words can express the wonderful love that was shed abroad in my heart. I wept aloud with joy and love.

That night, Finney woke up with doubts in his mind. Did these things occur? Had he really met the risen Lord? When the man got up the next morning, a third miraculous experience awaited him.

> Instantly the baptism I had received the night before returned to me. I scrambled to my knees in the bed and wept for joy. The Spirit seemed to say to me, "Will you doubt?" I cried, "No! I will not doubt! I cannot doubt!" It was no longer possible for me to doubt that the Spirit of God had taken possession of my soul.

As the lawyer worked that morning, waves of God's love washed over him. He shared the salvation message with his employer, who later committed his life to Christ. And, when his first client arrived, the attorney proclaimed, "Deacon, I have a retainer from the Lord Jesus Christ to plead His cause. I can no longer plead yours." With that, Charles Grandison Finney gave up practicing law and entered a life of service to the Lord.

Men such as Francis Asbury, Peter Cartwright, Timothy Dwight, and Lyman Beecher had led the way. In the 1820s, Charles Finney inherited the leadership of the spiritual awakening crossing the land. The excitement of western camp meetings and eastern church revivals had calmed down. But God did not want the Great Awakening to wither and die. He commissioned Charles Finney to fan the smoldering fire and rekindle the spiritual excitement.

At first, Finney studied under his pastor, George Gale. In March 1824, he was licensed to preach in the local area of the Presbyterian Church. A women's missionary society in western New York called him to minister in that area for three months. The thirty-two-year-old evangelist found himself traveling to a small town called Evans' Mills.

Curious townspeople attended Finney's service that first Sunday. Many of them were Unitarians. Finney preached the Gospel message in clear, understandable terms. He explained the concept of sin and the truth about Christ's death on the Cross. He admonished them to seek salvation and believe in the Lord Jesus Christ. After several weeks, the preacher realized nothing was changing. He would have to try something else.

It happened during an evening service. Orange and red streaks of light filtered through the schoolhouse windows. The congregation straggled into the school that doubled as a church on Sundays. School benches served as church pews and a podium had been set up front.

When everyone was seated, Finney began. "I've been here several weeks now," he stated wearily. "But I shall not stay much longer. There's no use." The preacher heaved a sigh as he inwardly grieved for the lost souls sitting in front of him. "I don't believe you want to receive the Gospel," he continued. "And so I don't need to stay. But I shall make one last call to salvation. If anyone here tonight would like to become a Christian, would you please rise?"

The stunned audience froze in their seats.

"Then you have rejected Christ and his Gospel," Finney thundered. "You are witnesses against one another, and God is witness against you all!"

The sanctuary erupted with commotion. People jumped to their feet. "Preacher, you must explain this!" roared one member. "That's right!" another exploded. When Finney refused, the congregation started to leave. Finney relented. "I'll preach once more, tomorrow evening," he announced.

The next day, threats of violence stalked the town. The preacher's behavior shocked everyone, even the handful of committed Christians. Only one Baptist deacon joined Finney to pray that God would have His way in the meeting that night.

That evening, people packed the meetinghouse. Finney opened the meeting with prayer. "Oh, Lord," he despaired, "they've hardened their hearts against You like a rock. Open their eyes to Your truth."

Finney recorded the following events in his journal:

> The Spirit of God came upon me with such power that it was like opening a battery (of heavy artillery) upon them. For more than an hour . . . the word of God came through me to them . . . . It was a fire and a hammer breaking the rock.

The evangelist never issued a call to confession and repentance that night. Instead, he preached again the following Sunday. This time, he directed his comments to the Unitarians, comparing the personal God of the Trinity to the impersonal god of Unitarianism. And this time, the word of God convicted them mightily. Almost everyone dedicated his life to Christ.

Throughout the small mill town, people turned to God. The revival spread through the countryside and neighboring villages. Soon, the awakening had reached all of western New York. The second wave of the Second Great Awakening was washing across America.

But Charles Finney had not yet been ordained. In July 1824, the ruling body of the church in that area (a presbytery) met to consider the proposal. But the Old School presbytery did not know what to make of all the new things Finney did which they called "new measures." For one thing, his preaching style was very different. He encouraged enthusiastic responses in his meetings, and he permitted women to pray aloud. The evangelist also preached every night, often permitting the meetings to run into the wee hours.

Most serious of all, Charles Finney spoke against the accepted doctrine of the day. He taught that sinners were not helpless, that they could choose to turn from their wicked ways. They could accept Jesus and enter the Kingdom of Heaven. They did not have to wait for God to do it for them. Despite their criticisms of him, however, the presbytery had to acknowledge the bulging membership rolls in the churches as a result of Finney's preaching. In the end, they decided to ordain him.

God's lightning storm of spiritual revival flashed across New York. Thousands of people came to Christ. Finney pushed across the state though he was often sick and exhausted. Soon, his fame spread throughout the northeast. God had anointed him. In 1831, nearly one-tenth of Rochester, New York, converted to Christianity. "The moral atmosphere of the city changed greatly," Finney wrote. "Taverns closed, crime decreased, and the jail stayed nearly empty for years afterward."

Finney's words were not the only thing transforming lives. His penetrating stare could propel a person into repentance. One time, the evangelist toured a textile mill near Utica, New York. Two girls, weaving at their looms, recognized him. They pointed at him and started giggling. The preacher glared at them but did not say a word. Immediately, their smiles vanished, and tears started rolling down their cheeks. Other women nearby reacted the same way. The owner of the mill stopped work. "It's more important for our souls to be saved than this factory to run," he announced to his employees. With that, Finney started a revival meeting, where almost every worker gave her life to Christ.

Utica became the center of Finney's ministry. The spiritual reawakening reached out from there like spokes running from the hub of a wheel. However, one young student from Hamilton College in Clinton, New York, wanted nothing to do with the evangelist. His name was Theodore Dwight Weld, son of a prominent New England minister.

Weld's natural leadership ability and gift of speaking captured his listeners. At the college, he constantly spoke against Finney and his "new measures" revival. But his aunt in Utica had been praying for his salvation. She finally persuaded Weld to promise to come to church with her one time.

On Sunday, Weld's aunt escorted him to a service. Little did the young man realize what God had in store. Unexpectedly, Charles Finney stepped up to the platform to preach. He chose for his text, "One sinner destroys much good." Weld squirmed and flinched but could not leave. He was sandwiched in the pew between his relatives. Against his will, the man sat and listened.

The next day, he encountered Finney outside a general store in Utica. With stinging words, Weld screamed at Finney and shook his fists. Curious shoppers crowded around to see what was going on. When the lad finally paused to catch his breath, Finney broke in.

"Mr. Weld," he uttered quietly, "are you the son of a minister of Christ? And is this the way for you to behave?"

At that, Weld stormed off. But within the hour, he appeared at Finney's door. "Doctor Finney, I beg forgiveness," the ashamed man said. "I was wrong, and I deeply regret what I've done."

The two men shook hands and talked. Their conversation ended after Finney offered a brief prayer for Weld. The following night, Finney's meetings began in Utica. Weld attended and confessed his wrongdoing before the entire congregation. Then he gave his life to Christ. From that time on, he devoted all his energy to promoting the revival.

Finney's ministry carried him from rural areas into major cities. In 1831, he preached a series of revival meetings in Rochester, New York. There, almost one-tenth of the people in the city were converted to Christ. About forty young men who had been converted in that revival entered the ministry.

Charles Finney preached to farmers and pioneers as well as to factory workers and professionals. He helped Americans rediscover their love of God. They realized their Heavenly Father yearned for them to love Him with all their hearts, souls, and minds. They discovered something else, too. Christianity meant loving one's neighbor. Whether a person was white or black, rich or poor, God Almighty had called His people to a covenant of love.

And here lies the importance of this Second Great Awakening. Finney and the other revivalist leaders urged Christians throughout the land to work toward making their country better. God's commandment to love one's neighbor included reforming society and abolishing its evils. Slowly but surely, the Body of Christ was realizing the evils of slavery. God was reforming their hearts and preparing them for the terrible storm just over the horizon.

Such a reformation meant work. And this meant that believers had to get involved. "The time has come," Finney urged, "for Christians to vote for honest men. God cannot sustain this free and blessed country unless the Church takes the right road. Politics are a part of religion in a country such as ours. Doing our duty to God requires us to help change America."

As the revival spread, Americans woke up to the importance of religion to the future of their nation. A people's faith anchors a country in solid moral principles. Without such an anchor, a nation can float anywhere and lose its way. But God wanted America to become a "city set on a hill."

The Christian Spectator, a nineteenth-century newspaper, summed it up like this: "What has religion to do with the State, you ask? . . . It operates as a controlling, purifying power in the consciences of the people. It is the last hope of republics."

In 1831, Lyman Beecher voiced his concern in his magazine, *The Spirit of the Pilgrims*. "The government of God is the only government which will hold society against depravity within and temptation without and this it must do by the force of its own law written upon the heart."

America, America, God shed His grace on thee. America had the foundation and the potential to lead the rest of the world. All that was required was for the revival to spread far enough and deep enough. If she could put her own house in order, God would use America to show the way to all other nations of the world.

But would she be able to do it? Slavery, sectional differences, economic greed, and the spirit of independence threatened to rip her apart. Would God continue to shed His grace from sea to shining sea?

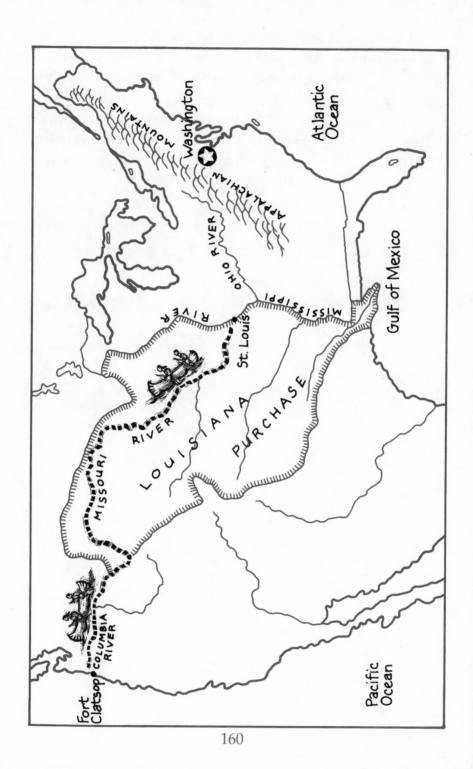

MOUNTAINS

Washington

Atlantic Ocean

APPALACHIAN

OHIO RIVER

MISSISSIPPI

Gulf of Mexico

RIVER

St. Louis

LOUISIANA

PURCHASE

MISSOURI

RIVER

Fort Clatsop

COLUMBIA RIVER

Pacific Ocean

CHAPTER
FOURTEEN

Thou has increased the nation O LORD...
Thou has extended all the borders of the land. (Isaiah 26:15)

"WAGONS, HO!"

As the population of the east coast soared, those with pioneering spirits pushed America's frontier farther west. At first, the rising tide of newcomers rushed over the Appalachian, Allegheny, and Great Smoky Mountain ranges, cutting roads and discovering passes. They carved new states that entered the Union. But America's thirst for land did not stop there.

In 1805, the Lewis and Clark expedition opened the country's eyes to the geographic marvels beyond the Mississippi. But before any settlers flocked west with their ox-drawn wagon trains and high hopes, long-haired, bearded adventurers known as mountain men were pushing west. Intent on trapping beaver, these wanderers embraced a life of independence in the endless mountains, grand plateaus, and rocky mountains across the Mississippi.

These rugged men were definitely a rare breed. Riding through the vast emptiness between the Missouri River and the Pacific, they kept one step ahead of civilization. Leather-skinned and grimy, they followed Indian trails and waded through mountain streams, setting traps for beaver. They roamed the great plains with the wandering herds of buffalo and wild horses. Alone and fancy-free, these frontiersmen grew calluses on their hearts as well as their hands. Cruelty marked their daily existence. Knives, tomahawks, and pistols were tucked inside the belts beneath their greasy leather shirts. Rifles lay across their saddles. The mountain men knew how to take care of themselves, but their worst enemy was the giant grizzly.

Chills ran down the two men's spines at the snarl of the grizzly. They watched in horror from behind a tree. The bear was big, almost eight feet tall, and it must have weighed 500 pounds. With pitchfork claws, the great brown beast seized their companion and hurled him to the ground like a sack of meal. In no time, he had gnarled the man's leg and ripped at his stomach. All at once, the animal raised up on its hind quarters and roared. The men covered their ears as the killer hunched over to nudge its lifeless prey. Sniffing to make sure the job was complete, the beast turned around and scampered back into the woods.

For a long time, the two mountain men clung to the safety of the tree. This had been their first encounter with a grizzly. They hoped it would be their last. With pounding hearts, they neared their companion.

"His heart's thumpin' but I'd say he's in bad shape," said the younger one. "Poor Hugh Glass. What should we do?"

"I reckon we need to stop the blood first," the other suggested, scratching his chin. "We're too far away to get him to Fort Kiowa. I fear he ain't long for this world."

The two men carried Glass to a nearby spring and washed his wounds. When the victim regained consciousness, they assured him they would remain with him until the end.

When Glass finally slipped into a coma two days later, the older man piped up, "Jim, let's get goin'. Ain't much use stayin' around, just to watch him die. He's as good as dead."

Jim Bridger hesitated before replying. "I guess you're right."

"No use leavin' his horse for them Injuns either," the first directed. "I'll fetch his rifle, too."

The men retrieved Glass's belongings, then gathered their supplies. After packing their horses, they mounted, glanced back, and trotted off.

Surprisingly, Glass came out of his coma. With blurred vision, he looked around for the others. They were nowhere to be found. For ten days, the wounded man kept himself alive by drinking spring water and scrounging wild berries. Then, with gritted teeth, he started crawling toward Fort Kiowa, a hundred miles away. To everyone's amazement, he made it. But he didn't stay long. He was going to find those men who had dumped him and stolen his gear. And he wasn't about to rest until he did.

On New Year's Eve, the mountain man caught up with Jim Bridger. Bridger's eyes bulged like balloons. How could this be? They'd left him for dead. Bridger's heart skipped a beat as he stammered, "Hugh Glass, you . . . you . . . you're alive!"

"Well, I ain't dead," Glass grunted, "and I want my stuff."

"We thought you was gone. We was only tryin' to do right."

Glass ended up forgiving Bridger because of his youth. After retrieving his rifle, he forgave the other man, too. But they'd best not mess with him again, and they'd better not steal his stuff!

What drew these bold adventurers to America's new frontier? It was "brown gold," as beaver pelts were known. As far back as the Pilgrims, trappers had traded beaver pelts because Europeans considered them very valuable. By the nineteenth century, trapping companies seriously competed with one another in the beaver country west of the Mississippi. Mountain men teamed up, meeting trading caravans once a year and swapping their pelts for alcohol, food, and whatever else they wanted. The caravans then traveled to market to sell their wares to merchants.

The annual rendezvous took place on a high plain near what is today Jackson Hole, Wyoming. It was like a rowdy, brawling carnival. Down from the mountains plodded each mountaineer, leading a mule or pack horse piled high with pelts. Nestled in the foothills, a makeshift city of tents housed every article a trapper might want. Fiddles, pianos, foul language, and whiskey highlighted each morning, noon, and night. The men had worked hard and wanted what they thought was a good time.

One particular trapper, however, stood out from this boisterous crowd. His name was Jedediah Smith. Gentle and quiet, this tall trapper never used bad language or tobacco or alcohol. Instead, he carried a Bible and prayed for the men, always trusting God to see them through hard times. And God did.

Jedediah loved to explore and headed up a number of explorations west of the Mississippi. In 1822, he joined the first trapping expedition up the Missouri. One day, he emerged from a thicket to surprise a grizzly. With a roar, the bear instantly grabbed him and broke his ribs. Then it clamped its jaws around Smith's head and dug its teeth into his skull. Shouts and shooting from the other trappers finally drove the beast off, but not before Smith had been badly wounded. With a dangling ear and blood gushing from his wounds, Smith remained calm, directing the men to wash his wounds and sew them up. The other trappers left while two men remained behind with Smith until help arrived.

Unfortunately, Indians discovered the camp and killed Smith's two companions. Alone and wounded, the starving explorer dragged himself from one beaver trap to the next, scrounging for food. Reading his Bible, the believer found encouragement in God's word. And God saw him through. Help came just in time. Before long, Smith was exploring again.

Not only was this gentle mountaineer the first to cross the Great Basin of present-day Nevada, he was also the first white man to explore the South Pass route through the Rockies to California. He was also the first to reach Oregon by traveling up the coast of California. Smith wrote journals of wonder at God's creations, marveling at sunbaked wood that looked like stone and the illusion of silvery lakes that vanished when anyone approached. God had given these spectacles to His children to enjoy.

Smith's greatest exploration started out as a trapping expedition for beaver, but it did not end up that way. One August 16, 1826, the party left Utah to head southwest through the valley of the Great Salt Lake. Smith described the land as "sandy plains and rocky hills, and once in twenty, thirty, or forty miles, a little pond or spring." Without water, the trappers did not find beaver, but they had gone too far and could not turn back. They grew edgy and quarrelsome. Soon, their supply of dried buffalo meat ran out. Yet, God supplied them with some corn and pumpkins planted by Indians, and the men did not starve. Tracking an old Indian trade route, the trappers crossed the Mohave Desert in southeastern California. Thirsty and tired, the men followed the Mohave River down the Sierra Nevadas and into the safety of the lush San Bernardino Valley on the Pacific.

Jedediah Smith died on an 1831 expedition to Santa Fe. The explorers had run out of water and fanned out to search for water holes. Smith spied one and rode to it, unaware that a band of Comanches hid nearby. In an instant, the Indians surrounded him and shot him. He was 32 years old.

God may have spared the young explorer a great disappointment. By 1834, the supply of beaver pelts was rapidly dwindling as more and more adventurers joined the ranks of the fur trappers. The fabled mountain men had to find something else to do. The answer lay just over the horizon, back east. Hundreds of canvas-covered wagon trains were about to roll through the prairie grasses and cross the mountain passes. These trains needed experienced guides. And who knew the new land to the west better than the mountain men?

It was a Great Migration, unlike any migration in the nation's history. And it began in 1823 with a New England schoolteacher named Hall Jackson Kelley. "The word came to me," he wrote, "to promote Christianity in the dark and cruel places about the shores of the Pacific." By 1829, Hall had established a society to encourage pioneers to move to places along the shores of Oregon.

In 1832, Nat Wyeth, departed from New England for Fort Vancouver. Two years later, he had returned to Boston and was ready to lead another group of pioneers to the far west. Jason Lee, a Methodist minister, preached the first American sermon west of the Rockies at Fort Hall. In September 1834, the travelers reached Vancouver and settled in nearby Willamette Valley. Lee urged the Methodist mission board back east to send families and teachers.

And the mission board did. In 1836, a missionary doctor named Marcus Whitman set out with his new bride and three others. The group planned to establish a mission in Oregon, and Whitman hoped to prove that loaded wagons could make it overland all the way to Oregon.

Guided by mountain man "Broken Hand" Fitzpatrick,

an entire caravan rumbled into the trading post at Fort Laramie in present-day Wyoming. Reluctantly, the doctor discarded his heavy farm wagon. Soon he discovered that even his smaller and lighter Dearborn bounced and creaked too slowly along the dusty, winding trails toward the Rockies. At Independence Rock, the settlers paused long enough to chisel their names into a stone. Later, thousands of immigrants would carve their names into the same stone that left a lasting memorial to the Great Western Migration.

On July 16, the wagons finally groaned into the rendezvous site at Green River. There, the Whitmans distributed Gospel tracts and Bibles to the crusty mountain men trading their pelts. Narcissa Whitman exclaimed with delight, "This is a cause worth living for!"

Soon the wagons pressed on, climbing higher and higher. At Soda Springs, the Whitman wagon broke its front axle. The doctor fashioned a two-wheeled cart out of the back half of the wagon. Gone was his dream of hundreds of wagons rolling across the land toward Oregon. Food grew scarce as the trail grew rockier. Gaunt and exhausted, the animals labored to pull the heavy loads. Whitman informed his wife they had to lighten the load. Tearfully, Narcissa wrote, "Poor little trunk. I am sorry to leave thee. Thou must abide here alone."

The little cart wobbled into Fort Boise, a trading post located at the junction of the Snake and Boise Rivers. On August 29, as the group camped 5,000 feet above sea level, they could see Mount Snow, 200 miles to the west. On September 1, 1836, they gobbled their breakfast and galloped down the slope to Fort Walla Walla on the Snake River in Washington. God had enabled them to travel 4,000 miles in just 6 months. The Whitmans established their mission town.

On March 14, 1837, Narcissa gave birth to Alice Clarissa Whitman, the first white American child born west of the Rockies. Four years later, Dr. Whitman's vision of wagon trains rolling west would come to pass. Seventy pioneers wheeled out of Saint Louis under the watchful eye of Broken Hand Fitzpatrick. In another two years, many trains and guides would follow. And one of the best was Jim Bridger.

Three trains of about a hundred wagons each gathered on the outskirts of Independence, Missouri. After months of dreaming and weeks of waiting, the families would soon be on their way west. The fertile soil of Oregon and California beckoned them with promises of new lives. Teams of mules and yoked oxen pulled the wagons into place. Men shouted and dogs yapped as the travelers organized themselves into a wagon train.

It was April of 1843. The travelers would have to wait a few moments longer before they could depart, however. Just to the west, a thunderstorm swept across the Great Plains, flattening the prairie grass with shrieking winds and stinging rains. Gophers huddled deep in their holes while a herd of buffalo madly stampeded across the spacious grassland in an effort to escape. As the storm reached the Missouri River, great streaks of lightning flashed through the black clouds, and explosions of thunder shook the earth.

"Joe, tether the oxen to the wagon!" one father screamed to his oldest son. "Joshua, you lash the flaps together."

"Matthew, I'll face the wagon into the wind while you pick up the loose gear," yelled another man. "Louise, you and Sarah calm the horses. Tell Rebecca to help your mother. Quickly now, the wind's picking up and the sky's getting dark!"

Panic swept through the train like the rising wind. But the guides, who had been through this before, stood by calmly, captivated by some hawks circling overhead. Such men as Broken Hand Fitzpatrick, Kit Carson, and Jim Bridger were already legends back East. They had journeyed to Oregon and back several times. They had crossed the Great American Desert. And now, they were taking others with them. America was heading westward.

The storm reached the train, drenching everyone. Then it passed. "Wagons, ho!" came the cry. Under Bridger's watchful eye, each wagon took its assigned place. Slowly a graceful line of white canvas uncoiled along the south bank of the Kansas River. They were on their way.

The train followed the Missouri River across a sweeping flatland stretching as far as the eye could see. The teamsters clutched the reins and cracked their whips. Squinting at the horizon in the distance, they let their minds wander. It really was a big sky up there, all blue and decorated by billowing white clouds. At night, the stars seemed so close you could almost touch them. Such a sky never hung over the narrow ridges and valleys of Connecticut. The drivers shouted at their teams. The wagons clinked merrily as swaying pots and pans played a symphony with the creaking wheels and the sound of oxen hooves.

Far ahead rode the tanned, weathered Jim Bridger, wearing his fringed leather coat and carrying his long-barreled rifle. Behind him, the caravan rumbled across the prairie grass. Days on the train followed a predictable routine, governed by the wagon master. As the sky lightened each morning around 4:00 A.M., lookouts fired their rifles. After a hot breakfast, the pioneers packed up their gear. Older boys prodded the oxen and mules into their harnesses as the adults made last minute arrangements. Then the wagons lined up for the bugle. At 7:00 A.M., the train stood ready to roll.

Slowly and steadily, the wagons stretched out across the prairie, kicking up storms of dust. The dust coated their clothes and food. It even stung their eyes, causing blindness for some. At midday, the wagon master selected a "nooning" site for a brief lunch stop. Then the bugle sounded again, and the broad wheels of the wagons began to turn across the earth once more. Weary wives sat up front as their husbands walked beside the animals. Younger children peeked out from the openings of the canvas or slept in the back. For their evening campsite, Bridger usually selected a watering hole or a trading post. The drivers wheeled their wagons into a hollow square, to guard against an Indian attack. And the campers prepared for supper and a long-awaited rest.

During the first weeks across the open plains, a train could usually cover as much as 15 to 18 miles. But, as the trail grew steeper, progress slowed down to 7 or 8 miles a day. "Keep moving!" ordered the wagon masters. The train had to stay on schedule, no matter what.

Tracking the north fork of the Platte River, the travelers marveled at Chimney Rock, towering 500 feet in the air. They trudged through the Badlands, hauling wagons and gear through steep slopes and huge, shimmering boulders. After leaving Fort Laramie, they carved their names on Independence Rock and entered the rough, rugged foothills of the Rockies.

"Haw! To the left now!" drivers commanded their teams. "Gee! To the right!" Slowly, the train labored up the winding, rocky trail toward the Continental Divide. Tugging and pulling, the animals strained under the load. Exhausted oxen fell to the ground, too weak to stand. Grief-stricken, the owners shot and butchered them. The train could not stop for anything. Animal skeletons from other trains grimly marked the trail. And so did the family heirlooms and prized bureaus of previous travelers.

"Move on!" the wagon master directed. Up, up, up, they went. The air turned thinner and cooler. The first snowfall lingered in the shadows ahead. They had to make it through the South Pass before another snow fell or they faced the horror of being trapped in the mountains for the winter. Everyone walked to save the horses, even the pregnant women. Following the Columbia River, the train crossed the Cascade Range. Pushing their belongings on rafts or in canoes, they headed downstream to Fort Vancouver. Oregon at last!

The Great Migration did not only record stories of triumph. Defeat, disappointment and even death marred the way for many pioneers. Two particular stories illustrate the high cost people paid for a nation yearning to stretch from sea to sea.

The first tragedy taught an invaluable lesson about following good advice. Two brothers from Illinois, George and Jacob Donner, packed up their families to head to California. By late summer of 1846, they had almost reached the South Pass. Instead of taking the known route, they listened to some bad advice and tried an untested shortcut. This shortcut, they were told, would save 400 miles. It left the main trail which everyone else took, at Fort Bridger and crossed the Wasatch Range. The Donner Expedition started their ascent without a guide, and the "shortcut" took them into an impassable gorge. They had to take a different route and lost much valuable time.

By October 30, the group had reached Truckee Lake, high in the Wasatch Range of the Sierras. Ahead lay Truckee Pass, the last major barrier between them and the Sacramento Valley in California. Had the train been on schedule, the pioneers might have made it. But it was cold now. Five feet of snow already clogged the treacherous pass, preventing them from moving on. Their dream turned into a nightmare. The Donners were trapped high in the mountains for the winter. With little food on hand, a rescue team of 17 people was sent on homemade snowshoes for help.

Snowstorms dumped 15 feet of snow on the lake. The desperate pioneers chewed on tree bark and animal hides. Half-crazy with hunger, they even ate the flesh of those who had died.

Meanwhile, the rescue team reached civilization and got help. On February 4, a relief expedition of Californians packed off to Truckee Pass. Two weeks later, they reached the lake to witness a horrible sight. Forty-seven weak, starving survivors meekly greeted them and told of their gruesome tragedy. It remained forever fixed in the minds of those traveling west.

Not all who went west did so willingly. Some were forced to go. The peaceful, law-abiding Cherokee Indians lived in the Southern Appalachians. Many of them farmed, raised cattle, and adopted the white man's ways. But neither the federal government nor the states recognized the rights given them under federal treaty. Angry Georgia citizens, hungry for more land, took matters into their own hands. They attacked the Indians and stole their land, and they demanded that the Georgia governor remove them from the state. In May 1838, he did just that.

U.S. Army troops rounded up every Cherokee man, woman, and child. They kicked in front doors and smashed windows. With bayonets and rifles, the soldiers herded the Cherokee together like animals. Because many of the Cherokee were Christians, they knelt in front of the soldiers, praying for Christ to have mercy on them. Leaving their homes and belongings, 15,000 brokenhearted Cherokee silently marched west. Carrying little more than their memories, the anguished tribe trudged helplessly toward Oklahoma. Hunger, sickness, and despair killed over 4,000 of them during the long, pitiful journey. It was truly a Trail of Tears, as it came to be known, and one of the saddest incidents in our nation's history.

Meanwhile, hundreds of pioneer wagons bounced and plodded west toward Oregon and California. Yet the biggest area of all was about to offer the greatest adventure of all—Texas!

CHAPTER

FIFTEEN

*Nevertheless, in Thy great compassion Thou didst not make
an end of them or forsake them, For Thou art a gracious and
compassionate God. (Nehemiah 9:31)*

"REMEMBER THE ALAMO!"

 In 1821, Mexico won its independence
from Spain and gained the Texas terri-
tory. This enormous panorama of
plains and open land lay between the
Sabine and Rio Grande rivers. At the
time, the ruthless Comanche Indians and a few
Mexicans occupied the area. The new republic decided to
offer land to foreigners. For the low price of $1.25 an acre,
Americans could emigrate there. The Mexican government
required only that the newcomers take an oath of alle-
giance to Mexico and embrace the Roman Catholic faith.
Other than that, they were on their own. Stephen Austin
and 300 colonists accepted the offer. With its fertile coastal
plain, Texas offered southerners an ideal area for growing
cotton. By 1830, over 20,000 American settlers had migrat-
ed to Texas. And thousands more were on their way.

But trouble was brewing within Mexico's political structure. New and unstable, the government cracked under
pressure from a political party, the Centralists, who seized
power in 1835. Immediately, the new party passed a law
forbidding any more people to move from the United

States. But it was too late to stop the flood of settlers. Mexico stationed troops in the territory to keep an eye on the frontier and the Texans. The Texans organized a militia of their own. The conflict in the territory heated to blazing hot.

Texas Governor Henry Smith and the Texas Council met at a place called Washington-on-the-Brazos. Stephen Austin, a colonel in the Texas militia, called all Texans to unite. "We must defend our rights, ourselves, and our country," he proclaimed.

When he said "our country," Austin was not referring to Mexico or the United States. He was talking about Texas. Broad and flat and desolate, the land belonged to them. They had forged a bond with it, and they would fight to keep it. Just as the colonists had stood for freedom 60 years before, the Texans were willing to stand again. Texas was theirs, and no one was going to steal it from them.

Santa Anna sent his brother-in-law, General Cos, across the Rio Grande to San Antonio to fortify the town. Soon, a small volunteer army of Texans assaulted the stronghold and won. Cos surrendered. In February 1836, an enraged Santa Anna stampeded across the border to storm San Antonio. He caught the celebrating Texans by surprise. They quickly retreated to the Alamo, an old Spanish mission near the San Antonio River.

For nearly two weeks, the stubborn band of 182 rebels held back Santa Anna's force of 4,000 Mexicans. Twice, enemy troops crashed against the walls of the tiny mission. But the sharpshooters rained musket fire and grapeshot on top of them, forcing them to retreat. Firing cannons from the top of the church, determined volunteers shelled the enemy and held off the attacks. Yet, the volunteers could not last forever. They were exhausted and running low on ammunition.

On March 3, Colonel Travis walked around the dusty ground of the Alamo, observing his men. Some squatted on dirt mounds, smoking cigars and waiting for the next siege. Other reloaded their rifles. A few watched the lizards and rats scurrying into their earthen homes. These men were all volunteers. Some, like Davy Crockett from Tennessee and Jim Bowie from Georgia, had traveled west to help the Texans' cause. Other mountain men had followed. Just the day before, 32 men from the fort at Gonzales had fought their way into the Alamo to stand with their countrymen. Yet, Travis knew it was only a matter of time. They needed reinforcements, the sooner the better.

Travis stamped the dust from his boots as he entered the wide wooden door of the old church. Slowly, he ventured toward his office, a room in the back. He scratched his scruffy beard as he sat down at a table near the window. Dusty and hot, the room looked stale and messy. Pieces of paper cluttered the dirt floor. In low spirits, the colonel pulled out another sheet. He had to get the words just right. For God's sake and for the sake of their country, the Texas Council had to send reinforcements.

A number of messengers had already stolen through enemy lines for help. Men like James Bonham had fled 92 miles to Goliad to plead with Colonel James Fannin. Travis had already sent one plea to the governor and the Council. On March 3, 1836, he decided to try one last time.

"The victory will cost the enemy so dear, that it will be worse for him than defeat," Travis wrote sorrowfully. "I hope your honorable body will send reinforcements. Our supply of ammunition is limited. God and Texas! Victory or death."

On the night of March 5, campfires dotted the courtyard of the Alamo. A handful of men gathered around, warming themselves against the cool March evening. No one spoke. They were exhausted beyond conversation. Ten days with nothing more than fitful sleep had taken its toll. As the haggard soldiers stared into the fire, a mournful trumpet solo floated through the night air. Santa Anna's band was playing that ancient song the Moors used in battle again. Night after night, the Mexican bands took turns blowing the same tune, *Deguello*. The haunting melody relentlessly pursued the tired men, even when it wasn't being played.

By the flickering firelight, the troops wrote letters that they knew would never be delivered. Tomorrow, it would all be over. The enemy had finally breached the north wall with its cannon. The Texans had filled the break with sandbags, but the enemy's cannon would open the hole again. Without reinforcements, the men inside the Alamo were doomed. They stared into the flames.

As March 6, 1836, dawned, columns of gray uniforms and plumed hats advanced on the old mission. Sharp bayonets glistened in the early morning sun. Behind the Mexican troops marched their bands, playing *Deguello*.

Boom! The one remaining cannon atop the rampart fired into the advancing column. Kentucky and Tennessee riflemen on the walls blazed at the enemy troops from the far range of 300 yards. Mexicans began to fall like butchered cattle. Stepping over their fallen comrades, more kept coming. The Texans snatched up their loaded rifles and fired again. Abruptly, the assault stopped. The Americans busied themselves reloading their rifles and leaning them carefully against the walls and within easy reach. Some sipped water from the water bucket while others fetched powder from the dangerously low powder keg. A few engaged in the humor of men who had fought well together, and knew they would soon die together.

"Ben, you're a disgrace to Kentucky, wasting ammunition that way," one sharpshooter chided another. "You ought to line up two of them Mexicans before you shoot, like I do."

"What're you talking about? Didn't you see that row of four go down in front of my column, right after the cannon stopped?" Ben jokingly replied.

"Hey, you two!" yelled another. "Stop flapping your gums, before you tucker yourselves out."

Suddenly, the dreadful sound of *Deguello*—the Mexican song that meant they would take no prisoners—drifted over the mission walls. The fight was on again! Stepping over fallen comrades, the Mexicans advanced. Closer and closer they marched until they pressed against the wall. Flinging their scaling ladders up, enemy troops started ascending like ants climbing a tree. But the Texas rifles spit too much lead and forced them to retreat.

"Yea!" From atop the rampart and behind the walls, the beleaguered American troops cheered.

But before long, the sound of *Deguello* floated through the air again. This time, the Mexicans struck all four walls at once. Heaving their scaling ladders against the stone, hundreds of troops scrambled up. Without time to reload, the Texas rebels slammed rifle butts into the faces of those reaching the top first. More Mexicans poured into the compound. Using their tomahawks and Bowie knives, the defenders slashed and hacked away at the enemy, determined to kill as many as they could. Bloodcurdling screams saturated the morning air as Mexicans and Texans crumpled to the ground. Even Jim Bowie, bedridden in the old church, killed two Mexicans with a pistol hidden under his blanket before they shot him.

When it was over, the Mexican soldiers mutilated the bodies of the Texans. Then they withdrew. But Santa Anna had paid a high price for his victory. He lost 1,600 troops, and he created a powerful, rousing legend. "Remember the Alamo!" echoed between the boulders and across the plains in Texas. The small band of heroes who had fought and died for liberty would not be forgotten.

Santa Anna marched northeast toward Goliad. Despite an order to blow up the fortress and retreat, Colonel Fannin and his 500 troops lingered at the fort. When Mexican troops broke across the horizon, the colonel decided to run for it and escape across the prairie. But a superior Mexican force easily hemmed the Texans in and killed them.

Then a dual battle cry cut across the prairies. "Remember the Alamo!" and "Remember Goliad!"

The air along the San Jacinto River hung hot and still that noon of April 21, 1836. After a cooked meal, most of the Mexican army lay fast asleep in whatever shade they could find. Even the sentries leaned against trees or propped themselves up with their muskets, listening to the drone of the crickets. Santa Anna had permitted them a well-earned siesta today. For nearly seven weeks, the troops had been chasing General Sam Houston and his retreating band of Texas rebels. Finally they had cornered them at Galveston Bay, near the San Jacinto River. It was time to rest.

Three-quarters of a mile away in the Texas ranks, the exact opposite was taking place. At three o'clock that afternoon, General Houston, commander in chief of the Texas militia, was rounding up his troops. Sitting atop his white charger, Saracen, the general watched his troops.

"Calvary to the right!" he ordered, waving a gloved hand in one direction. "Keep the Mexicans from breaking across the prairie. Texas regulars, in the middle! That's right. You'll be flanked by our two gifts from Cincinnati, the twin sister cannons."

Houston's stallion shifted his weight as the general yelled his commands. He held onto the saddle horn with his left hand. "Now, you riflemen from Kentucky and Tennessee, move left! Foot soldiers, form into a single line stretching from the river to the bayou. Hold your fire till you can make it count!" he ordered.

The general then drew his sword and pointed at the distant rise in the plain. "Forward . . . Texas!"

Bearded and grimy, the long line of Texans stomped across the open plain. With rifles leveled and ready, the men advanced. Incredibly, the Mexican sentries did not spot them until they were within rifle range. The shrill blast of enemy bugles howled a frantic alarm. Instantly, the Texans shifted from a walk to a trot. Panicked, the Mexicans desperately tried to form into columns.

Enemy sentries fired their muskets. Down went Houston's white charger. The general scrambled to his feet and thrust his sword forward. At once, the Texans broke into a run. "Remember the Alamo!" they cried in deafening tones. The Mexican troops froze in horror.

At twenty yards, the Americans opened fire and then demolished the Mexican barricades. Like a swarm of bees, they stormed into the enemy's camp. "Remember the Alamo!" came the shout again and again as they waded into the confused sea of Mexicans. Bump! Thud! Rifle butts and even tomahawks slammed into enemy heads. And now the cries of the Americans were triumphant! They knew they were going to win!

Houston's second horse went down. This time a musket ball hit his ankle and his boot filled with blood. Still he pressed on. Within twenty minutes, the Mexicans broke, fleeing for their lives. But they had no place to go! The waiting Texas cavalry cut down those escaping to the prairie, and the militia rounded up and shot those withdrawing to the bayou. By sunset the Mexican army had surrendered.

Six hundred thirty Mexican bodies littered the San Jacinto battlefield. Two hundred more lay wounded. Texan losses amounted to two men killed in action and twenty-four wounded.

The next day, a Texan patrol spied someone dressed in a

blue cotton dress, leather cap, and red felt slippers. They dragged the strange figure into camp for questioning. "El Presidente!" the Mexican prisoners murmured as the figure passed by. The Texans eyed one another with surprise and delight.

"General," the aide rushed in, panting. "We have him, sir. Santa Anna! He's right outside!"

General Houston tried to prop himself up on his cot. He looked outside the flap of the tent. One of his patrols held an odd-looking character in a dress. "Escort him in, Sergeant," the general ordered.

The soldiers ushered the Mexican general into the tent. The black-haired Mexican stared at the Texan coldly. With his hands bound, he stood stiffly and did not say a word.

"We meet at last," General Houston commented under his breath. Turning to his interpreter, he said. "Tell the General these are the terms of the armistice. He will order his troops out of Texas, to the other side of the Rio Grande. And he will sign a treaty of Texas independence."

The flag with the lone star on it began flying over the Republic of Texas. News of the astounding victory reached the city of Washington. Immediately, the question of Texas's annexation turned into a debate over the issue of slavery. Southern planters favored admitting Texas because it could produce cotton. Northern abolitionists opposed this as a power play by the south. Once again, Congress avoided the underlying issue. Rather than annex Texas, it passed a bill recognizing Texas's independence.

On March 3, 1837, less than 24 hours before leaving office, President Jackson signed the bill. That evening, he invited the Texas representatives to the White House to celebrate. At the stroke of midnight, he raised his glass. "Gentlemen," he toasted, "the Republic of Texas."

The President's buggy vibrated as it approached Capitol Hill. With a jolt, it lurched to the left, swerving to miss a broken limb in the middle of the road. Inside, a white-haired Andrew Jackson clutched a hanging yellow rope for balance. He stared out the curtained window, waiting patiently to arrive. He was going to Congress to deliver his last official speech as President of the United States. It was March 4, 1837.

The carriage arrived at the Capitol building in plenty of time. Already, senators and representatives piled into the House chamber for the joint session. Dressed in a white, high-necked, ruffled shirt, black topcoat, and breeches, the President looked striking. He emerged from the buggy and proceeded up the steps into the building. After shaking many hands and bidding farewell to a number of admirers, he entered the House chamber. Listening to the applause due him as President, Jackson walked down the aisle toward the Speaker's bench.

It's been a good eight years, he thought with satisfaction as he neared the platform. *We've accomplished a lot. Americans are moving west like never before, to Texas, California, and Oregon. New roads are making traveling easier, foreign trade's increasing, and we've paid off the national debt. Yep, it's been a good eight years.*

Jackson sat down to wait for the introduction. Upon rising, he fished some small, gold-rimmed glasses from his coat pocket and put them on. The President cleared his raspy voice.

"Mr. Speaker and esteemed members of Congress, you have the highest of human trusts committed to your care," he said pointedly. "Providence has showered on this favored land blessings without number, and has chosen you as the guardians of freedom, to preserve it for the benefit of the human race."

Peering through his glasses, Jackson looked at the distinguished body sitting before him. One common cord bound them together. Though many, they were one nation, a nation under God.

"May He who holds in His hands the destinies of nations, make you worthy of the favors He has bestowed, and enable you . . . to guard and defend to the end of time the great charge He has committed to your keeping."

Jackson's final speech challenged Americans to remember Who had commissioned them and what He expected. They were one nation under God, called together to create His kingdom on earth. The Pilgrims and Puritans had carried this vision to the New World. The American colonists had fought for it during the War for Independence. The Founding Fathers had incorporated it into the new government. With God's Word at the heart of their society's life, they could truly become a "city set on a hill" for all the world to see.

But this attitude of humility must continue. To recognize the sinfulness of their ways meant acknowledging the sovereignty of God, not only in their personal affairs but in the affairs of the whole nation. God held their destiny in His hands, but it was up to them to preserve the freedoms.

Yet, something had changed. Americans seemed to be losing their sense of dependence on Divine Providence. Why? They had fallen in love with the glorious, beautiful continent known as North America. And they wanted as much of it as they could get. In 1838, John L. O'Sullivan, a New York editor, summed it up this way. "(It is) the right of our manifest destiny to overspread and possess the whole of the continent which Providence has given us for the development of the great experiment of liberty . . . entrusted to us."

Manifest destiny—the old Puritan vision of a "city set on a hill"—once again stirred the imaginations of Americans everywhere. At this point, however, the "city" included the entire North American continent. For many, patriotic pride had eclipsed Christian humility. From east to west, from north to south, it seemed obvious that the United States should control it all. Why? Because Americans thought God intended her to have it.

Jackson's last speech reminded America of what God expected. Yet, one obstacle lurked ahead like a snake in the path. Three million souls remained shackled by the bondage of slavery.

CHAPTER
SIXTEEN

[If] My people who are called by My name humble themselves and pray, and seek My face and turn from their wicked ways, then I will hear from heaven, will forgive their sin, and will heal their land. (2 Chronicles 7:14)

SOUNDING THE TRUMPET

The morning of August 22, 1831, dawned quietly in the Virginia Tidewater country. A gray mist rose off the water. Songbirds greeted the sun, and crickets chirped in the fields. The crops were out, and in another month the heavy work of harvesting would begin. On this day, many of the white farmers were gone. They had hitched up their teams and taken their families south to the camp meetings in North Carolina.

The thought of this brought a smile to the face of a particular Negro slave. He had been waiting for a sign. As Nat Turner carefully ran his thumb over the edge of his razor-sharp field knife, he noticed the sun was colored by a strange bluish tinge. This was his sign. It was time to carry out his plan.

His plan—Nat had gone over it and over it in his mind. For years, he had carefully nurtured it like a new seedling, feeding it so it would grow. His visions had helped. The spirits had appeared to him many times while he had fast-ed and meditated in the woods. They had told him what to do. It was such a simple idea. With seven, trusted black friends, he would slaughter every white in the county. Then other blacks would rise up, and together they would all march to the armory in Jerusalem, the county seat. After stealing all the weapons, they could lose themselves in Dismal Swamp, just 30 miles away. The whites would never find them, and more Negroes could join them. Yes, this was the perfect way to exact God's vengeance on the whites.

Turner summoned his men. As the morning sun burned off the mist, they silently crept into the Travis household. The Travis family owned Nat Turner and lived in Southampton County, west of Norfolk. With sharp knives and even sharper precision, the slaves killed the Travises and stole to the next plantation, where more slaves joined them. Altogether they raided three plantations before they reached the Blounts' house. There, old Dr. Blount rallied his slaves to fend off the killers.

By the end of the second day, Turner's force numbered about 70. It had murdered 55 white men, women, and children. With each success, Nat grew more confident that his plan would succeed. But it was an obvious scheme, and every white man in the county knew exactly where the slaves were headed. A few miles outside Jerusalem, the state militia overtook the slaves. In the bloody fight that followed, the blacks fled into the swamps. Seeking revenge, the whites chased them down and shot them. Turner escaped. For two months, white patrols scoured the byroads and combed the swamps. At last, they apprehended the bandit. His swift trial resulted in a sentence of death by hanging.

Virginia breathed a collective sigh of relief. But the Nat Turner rebellion had damaged the south far more than they realized. Like the first rumbling of an oncoming train, the revolt awakened the south to the danger of slave insurrections, and slave owners hardened their hearts toward blacks.

In December 1831, the Virginia House of Delegates assembled to debate the issue. The entire nation watched as Virginia once again led the way. What would the south do about its slaves since the Turner Rebellion? Journalists and on-lookers packed the gallery seats in the hall as the legislators filed in. Some of the most eloquent men in America would present the case, pro and con. Men such as Thomas Marshall, eldest son of the Chief Justice, and Thomas Jefferson Randolph, favorite grandson of the third President, slowly walked down the aisles to their seats.

Should Virginia emancipate its slaves? And if she did, where would they go? Back to Africa? Who would pay to send them? For that matter, who would pay the white slave owners for their loss? These were the questions facing the Virginia delegates.

The forces erupted on both sides. Thomas Marshall rose to his feet to condemn slavery. "It ruins whites as well as blacks. It effectively does away with the middle class, leaving only the very rich and the very poor."

Alexander Knox of Mecklenburg County countered, "But it is not evil. To the contrary, I consider it beneficial!"

The gallery gasped. No one had ever publicly declared

that slavery helped society. But now the ground was broken. Others quickly followed suit, and a new wave of thinking bubbled to the surface of everyone's mind.

James Gholson of Brunswick County stood up. "The slaves of Virginia are as happy as any laboring class in the world. They are content today and have no care or anxiety for tomorrow."

"Whether it is a blessing or a curse," John T. Brown asserted, "we cannot free ourselves from it. Slavery was forced on us by a train of events that could not be controlled.

"Where is it written that slavery is so wrong? Even the Savior of mankind did not condemn it. I contend that the happiness of the slave does not call for emancipation . . . . Man must be civilized and enlightened before he is fitted to enjoy liberty!"

People sitting in the House gallery interrupted Brown with loud murmurs. He continued. "The greater part of mankind must . . . be poor and ignorant, toiling anxiously for their daily bread. All cannot be raised to the top of the scale . . . Whatever evils may flow from slavery, it would now be a far greater evil to abolish it."

Brown had said it. He claimed that the Negro was happy in his lot, happier than most men. Slaves could not handle freedom if they received it. Slavery might be evil, but it was not a sin.

Yet others like Thomas Randolph argued that it was a sin. "Mr. Brown appeals to the Christian religion to justify his position. What part of the Scripture does he use? Is it the part that teaches charity, justice, and good will to all?

Or that which teaches that you do unto others as you would have them do unto you?"

The debates dragged on for seven weeks, and it seemed as if nothing happened. Yet something had. For the first time, the south openly accepted the idea that slavery did not have to be done away with. Slaveholders were beginning to claim that it was a positive good. They no longer had to soothe their guilty consciences. They blindly accepted the argument that Scripture was on their side. They ignored the reality that the south was growing poorer by the decade. They dismissed the growing concern from other parts of the country. And they discounted the fact that the other Christian nations, including England, had outlawed the practice. They believed that all men were created equal, but they couldn't let themselves believe that this meant blacks as well. Hadn't God created them unequal? That was the way life was.

But what about the north? As the south shifted its thinking, so did the north. Only the north was pointing the opposite way. William Lloyd Garrison, a strong opponent of slavery, galvanized readers in the north with his newspaper, the *Liberator*. "Slavery has fouled the land with its stench!" he proclaimed. "We must emancipate the slaves now!" The editor attacked the Constitution itself as a "covenant with death and an agreement with hell" because it protected slavery. He urged abolitionists to cry out for secession from the "diseased" south.

Southern states recoiled in horror at Garrison's vicious attacks. Mississippi even passed a law offering a reward of $5,000 for the arrest and conviction of anyone circulating the *Liberator* within its borders. But northerners were listening to Garrison. While many still regarded him and his colleagues as troublemakers, their crusade against slavery was beginning to take effect.

Another abolitionist leader contributed to this growing movement for reform. His name was Theodore Dwight Weld, the young man once converted by Charles Finney. Weld emphasized the religious nature of the struggle against slavery. "Slavery is a sin," he declared. "It crushes the body, tramples . . . the intellect, breaks the heart, and kills the soul." Weld pictured the struggle in its ultimate terms. The battle was not against flesh and blood. It was against the powers and principalities of darkness. It was a war in the heavens. And its outcome would decide whether America would ever fulfill her divine calling.

In 1837, a single event forced northerners to recognize what was going on. A mob descended on the office of Elijah P. Lovejoy, a prominent antislavery editor, in Alton, Illinois. When Lovejoy ran out to protect his presses, the mob killed him and dumped his equipment in the Mississippi. For the first time, a white man had been murdered because of slavery.

Lovejoy's death electrified the north. Men in Boston wept openly. Abolitionists held protest meetings. And one particular man vowed to dedicate his life to destroying slavery. After listening to Lovejoy's brother describe the editor's last days, a lean, narrow-faced man stood up in the back of a church in Hudson, Ohio. John Brown raised his right hand as if taking an oath. "Here, before God, in the presence of these witnesses," he declared, "I consecrate my life to the destruction of slavery." Over the next 20 years, Brown's attempts to raid southern settlements and free the slaves would help bring on the war.

On March 3, 1837, the Illinois Assembly passed a resolution against abolition societies. One tall, young assemblyman refused to vote for this resolution. Twenty-eight-year-old Abraham Lincoln believed that America stood for freedom and equality. Although not an abolitionist, the lawyer from Springfield believed that slavery was evil, and he wanted others to realize it, too. Twenty-three years later, Abe Lincoln would become the sixteenth President of the United States. He would help end slavery and would lead the fight to preserve the Union during the greatest crisis in American history.

Another northerner was learning the ugly realities of slavery as well. In 1837, Harriet Beecher Stowe, the daughter of Lyman Beecher, watched mobs in Cincinnati wreck the press of James Birney, an antislavery editor, and pull down the houses of respectable free blacks. Two years later, her husband and her brother, Henry Ward Beecher, would rescue her free black maid from those who wanted to sell her into slavery. The next year, whites would attack the black quarters in town, murdering men, raping women, and kidnapping children. Mrs. Stowe developed strong views about slavery.

One day, Mrs. Stowe received a note from her sister-in-law. "Now, Hattie, if I could use a pen as you can, I would write something that would make this whole nation feel what an accursed thing slavery is." Harriet Beecher Stowe decided to do just that. In 1851, *Uncle Tom's Cabin* appeared and sharply divided the nation. Americans read about a kindly old slave, named Uncle Tom, who was sold downriver to the brutal overseer, Simon Legree. They cried as he was beaten to death for refusing to betray two fellow slaves. Their hearts reached out as the Negro girl, Eliza, escaped across the frozen Ohio River clutching her baby. Within the first year, the book sold 300,000 copies. And America woke up to the horrors of slavery.

As the reform movement to abolish slavery swept across the north, the south looked for a spokesman. It found one in South Carolina Senator John C. Calhoun, former Vice President under Jackson. In 1837, the southerner took the Senate floor to deliver the most crucial address of his career.

"They who imagine the (abolitionist) spirit abroad in the north will die away . . . have formed a very inadequate concept of its real character," the thin, wirey-haired southerner shouted. "We are (resting on) a volcano! The present generation of northerners are being taught to hate the people and institutions of nearly one half of this Union."

Calhoun paused. "It is easy to see the end," he sadly resumed. "We must become two people . . . Abolition and Union cannot coexist."

That same year, some Christians wondered how much longer God would continue to shed His grace on America. Few of them anticipated a nationwide day of judgment, when God's wrath would fall on both the north and the south, but it came. The country could have avoided the disaster. Congress could have treated the issue of slavery as a national crisis. It could have abolished the slave trade.

Religious leaders could have cried out against the injustice instead of working with it. And the nation could have turned to God. Sadly enough, however, America did not do any of these. Instead, she slipped further and further down the bank toward civil war.

Yet, God honored His covenant with the Founding Fathers and preserved His plan for the nation during the 50 years following the Constitutional Convention in Philadelphia. Through pioneers and presidents, mountain men and circuit riders, God weaved the tapestry of His will into America's life. He expanded her borders from one sea to another. He laid the groundwork for a nation of law. He held the country together in spite of depression and war. And He forced the nation to accept the ugly reality of the evils of slavery. America was still His new Israel.

God's covenant with our forefathers endures today. He is still holding before us the opportunity to shine Christ's light to a dark world. But it is a great task. Our nation may lose God's blessings if we don't change our ways. There are so many of our citizens who are doing wrong things; illegal drugs murder many of our young people, abortion kills thousands of unborn babies each year. People don't believe the Bible. They search for truth elsewhere. Many people are greedy, spending money they don't have and encouraging the government to do the same thing. Racial hatred and violence tear apart our cities and our hearts. The ideal of brotherly love is forgotten as people look out only for themselves and deliberately disobey God's Word.

Yet, God is still God, the Lord of all history. And He tells us the way out of this mess. He says that His followers must turn back to Him:

> [If] My People who are called by My name, humble themselves and pray, and seek My face and turn from their wicked ways, then I will hear from heaven, will forgive their sin, and will heal their land.
>
> (2 Chronicles 7:14)

God's people must lead the way to turn our country around. We must turn away from our selfishness and disobedience. We must learn to love other people and be concerned for their needs. We must stand up for all that the Bible teaches, even when people make fun of us for doing it. And we must answer God's call to live in obedience to Christ.

God is asking all of His people to do whatever we can in our own homes, neighborhoods, schools, and cities to spread God's Word, to encourage people to live together in peace, and to protect those who cannot protect themselves. Throughout America's history, God has used individuals to bring about change. He will do that today through us, if we are committed to serving and obeying Him. Then when we sing about our country we can have hope for the future, just as it says in the song:

> *America! America!*
> *God shed His grace on thee,*
> *And crown Thy good with brotherhood*
> *From sea to shining sea.*

GLOSSARY

abolitionist (n)—a person who wanted to abolish slavery

acquit (v)—to find innocent and to set free

advocate (v)—to argue for a particular side or cause

ambassador (n)—a person appointed by one country to
  represent it to another

aristocrat (n)—a member of the nobility

Badlands (n)—a section of barren land in southwestern
  South Dakota and northwestern Nebraska

battery (n)—a military fortification equipped with cannon

brig (n)—a two-masted ship with square sails

buccaneer (n)—a pirate

class-conscious (adj)—aware of belonging to a particular
  class in the social order

collateral (n)—something of value which a borrower gives
  to assure that a loan will be repaid

commission (n)—a document authorizing someone to per-
  form certain duties

counterfeit (adj)—phony; not the real thing

coup (n)—a sudden, successful action

deception (n)—a cunning or sneaky act

deism (n)—the belief in an impersonal God who created the
  world but left people to work things out on their own

earthwork (n)—a fortification made by piling up soil

electoral (adj)—having to do with an election

enlightenment (n)—the eighteenth-century European philosophy centering on one's ability to reason rather than dependence on God

frigate (n)– fast, medium-sized sailing warship

gorge (n)—a deep, narrow pass between steep banks

hemp (n)—a tall plant known for its tough fiber and used to make rope or sailcloth

hoecake (n)—a thin bread made of cornmeal

Huguenot (n)—a French Protestant

hypocrisy (n)—pretending to be what someone is not

impress (v)—to force men to serve in the military

indigo (n)—a group of plants that yield a blue dye

insurrection (n)—rebellion

intervention (n)—any interference in the affairs of others

Jacobins (n)—members of a revolutionary party, which started in France during the Revolution of 1789

larboard (n)—the left-hand side of a ship

mar (v)—to damage or spoil

morale (n)—confidence, enthusiasm

nullification (n)—the act of declaring a federal law null and void

parcel (n)—a piece or portion

partnership (n)—a business arrangement entered into between two or more individuals

persecution (n)—being harassed or oppressed

prostrate (adj)—lying flat

rabble-rousing (adj)—stirring up the masses of people

rampart (n)—an embankment of earth used to defend or protect

redoubt (n)—an advance fortification used to secure hilltops or the flanks of entrenchments

relentlessly (adv)—persistently

rendezvous (v)—to meet at an agreed time and place

renegade (n)—a traitor or turncoat

revival (n)—the conversion of many people to faith in Christ in a given country or area is changed for the better

rift (n)—a difference of opinion

risers (n)—a platform built in stairsteps for better viewing

rogues (n)—scoundrels and criminals

rudderless (adj)—floating without a rudder or that part of the ship used to steer

secession (n)—formal separation

tonnage (n)—the weight of a ship in tons

Unitarians (n)—those who deny the Trinity by believing that God is a single being

volley (n)—the discharge of a number of weapons at the same time or in quick succession

STUDY QUESTIONS

Chapter 1   **In God's Plan**

1. In what year did the first slaves arrive on America's shore?
    a) 1610
    b) 1615
    c) 1619
2. What group of English settlers sailed to the New World to establish a Bible-based society?
3. England settled _____ colonies along the East Coast during the late 1600s and early 1700s.
4. Why did the delegates at the Constitutional Convention have so much trouble agreeing? What did Benjamin Franklin say to change their thinking?

Chapter 2   **Heading West**

1. Why did Caleb Hotchkiss and his family leave New England to head west? Did they want to go?
2. The Northwest Territory eventually became what five states?
3. Give three reasons the pioneers headed west.
4. How does the Story of Stone Soup illustrate the Yankee's resourceful ways?
5. Name two ways the pioneers of the early 1800s differed from their Puritan forefathers.

Chapter 3   **Revival**

1. What particular town in Kentucky attracted criminals? Why?
2. The name of the Presbyterian preacher who preached the gospel in Rogues Harbor was _____
3. Why did God begin to pour out His Spirit on McGready's congregation?
4. How many people showed up for the Cane Ridge Revival? Why as this important?
5. Name two famous Methodist circuit riders.

Chapter 4   **The Second Great Awakening**

1. Where did the revival of the 1800s begin in New England?
2. Explain the main difference between the American War for Independence and the revolution going on in France.
3. Who were the French Jacobins?
4. (T/F) God's Holy Spirit touched the hearts of New England in the same way He touched the frontiersmen.
5. What two famous men led the revival in New England during the early 1800s?

Chapter 5   **The Louisiana Purchase**

1. What country owned the Louisiana Territory in 1803?
2. Why did Napoleon want to sell this territory to the United States?
3. In 1804, the Lewis and Clark expedition set off from _____ and ended in _____
4. What was the purpose of their exploration?

Chapter 6   **Chief Justice**

1. Who was the fourth Chief Justice of the United States Supreme Court?
2. Name three character traits that endeared him to every one.
3. In what famous case did Chief Justice Marshall declare that the Constitution was the supreme law of the land?
4. What was John Marshall's vision for the country?

Chapter 7   **"Don't Give Up the Ship!"**

1. Why was Britain forcing American sailors to serve on British ships?
2. Did the Embargo Act force England to cooperate? Why or why not?
3. Why did America focus on Canada at the beginning of the war?
4. What kind of man was Lieutenant Oliver Perry? How did he differ from Captain Elliott?

Chapter 8   **The Dawn's Early Light**

1. What were privateers?
2. How did God use the weather to stop the British from destroying the capital?
3. Describe the British assault on Baltimore in your own words.

Chapter 9   **The Era of Good Feelings**

1. Name three problems facing the nation during the Era of Good Feelings.
2. Describe United States relations with Spain during this period.
3. John Quincy Adams negotiated the Transcontinental Treaty with Spain. What did this treaty do?
4. How did Adams help preserve God's plan for the nation?

Chapter 10   **A House Dividing**

1. Look up Matthew 12:25. How does this Scripture apply to America during the nineteenth century?
2. Do you think God's hand was behind Eli Whitney's invention of the cotton gin? Why or why not?
3. How did the cotton gin revolutionize the South?
4. Describe the daily work of a slave in the South.
5. What was the Missouri Compromise?

Chapter 11   **A Fire Bell in the Night**

1. The Reverend Jeremiah Jeter decided to keep his slaves. Why?
2. How were southerners trapped by the system of slavery?
3. What was the fundamental heart difference between the North and the South?

Chapter 12   **Liberty and Union Forever!**

1. God preserved His plan through three great national leaders. Who were they?
2. Discuss the character traits of Andrew Jackson.
3. How did Andrew Jackson help preserve the Union?
4. What was the policy of nullification?

Chapter 13   **A Lightning Storm of Revival**

1. What important role did Charles Finney play in the Second Great Awakening?
2. How did Finney's preaching style differ from the style of his day?
3. What was the spiritual importance of the Second Great Awakening?

Chapter 14   **"Wagons, Ho!"**

1. Who were the mountain men? What drew them to the American frontier?
2. One of the most famous of these mountain men was

    _____

3. In 1823, Hall Jackson Kelly had a vision for the shore of the Pacific. What was his vision?
4. Why did the wagon trains traveling west have to keep a tight schedule?

Chapter 15   **"Remember the Alamo!"**

1. Why did Mexico's policies enrage the Texans?
2. What price did Santa Anna pay for his victory at the Alamo?
3. How did the battle at Galveston Bay differ from the fight at the Alamo?
4. What did the term "manifest destiny" mean?

Chapter 16   **Sounding the Trumpet**

1. Name 2 ways the Nat Turner rebellion damaged the South.
2. In 1837, what single event jolted America into recognizing the problem of slavery?
3. Read 2 Chronicles 7:14. What will God do if we obey this verse? How can you obey this Scripture?